A Peculiar History

Sabotage, Sedition and Sundry Acts of Rebellion

A Peculiar History

The Middle Passage

Sabotage, Sedition and Sundry Acts of Rebellion

Slavery and the Forging of Early America

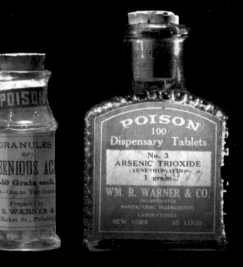

A Peculiar History

Sabotage, Sedition and Sundry Acts of Rebellion

David Aretha

MORGAN REYNOLDS
PUBLISHING

www.morganreynolds.com

Greensboro, North Carolina

To join the discussion about this title, please
check out the Morgan Reynolds Readers Club
on Facebook, or Like our company page to stay
up to date on the latest Morgan Reynolds news!

Cover: An 1862 photo taken by Civil War photographer Timothy
H. O'Sullivan at J. J. Smith's plantation near Beaufort, South
Carolina. The enslaved on this cotton plantation were among the
first to be liberated after President Abraham Lincoln issued his
preliminary Emancipation Proclamation on September 22, 1862.

A Peculiar History

Sabotage, Sedition and Sundry Acts of Rebellion

Copyright © 2015 by Morgan Reynolds Publishing

Library of Congress Cataloging-in-Publication Data

Aretha, David.
 Sabotage, sedition, and Sundry acts of rebellion / by David Aretha.
    pages cm. -- (A peculiar history)
 Includes bibliographical references and index.
 ISBN 978-1-59935-406-4 -- ISBN 978-1-59935-407-1 (e-book) 1. Slave
insurrections--United States. 2. Slave insurrections--North
America--Juvenile literature. I. Title.
 E447.A74 2014
 306.3'620973--dc23

                          2013016550

Printed in the United States of America
First Edition

Book cover and interior design by:
Ed Morgan, navyblue design studio
Greensboro, NC

CONTENTS

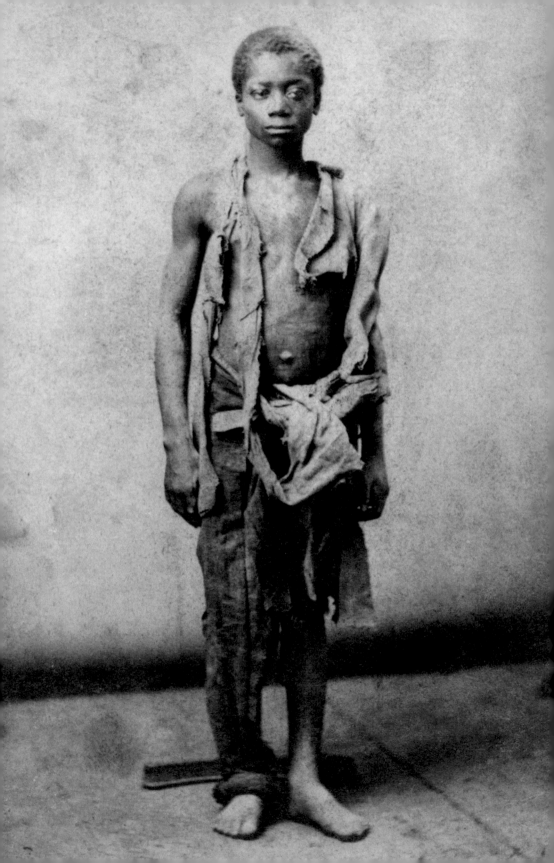

OUR PECULIAR INSTITUTION

In American history, the phrase "peculiar institution" refers to slavery. The origin of the phrase is not clear, but in 1828 and 1830 John C. Calhoun used "peculiar institution" in his speeches and writings. A leading proponent of slavery, Calhoun argued that the Declaration of Independence is in error when it states that "all men are created equal." Frenchman Alexis de Tocqueville refers to the "peculiar institution" in his nineteenth century narrative about his travels in America, and Stephen Douglas, in his last debate with Abraham Lincoln on October 15, 1858, comments on the peculiar institution.

By the 1830s, the euphemism was widely used, by both defenders of slavery and abolitionists:

> "Talk about slavery! It is not the peculiar institution of the South. It exists wherever men are bought and sold, wherever a man allows himself to be made a mere thing or a tool, and surrenders his inalienable rights of reason and conscience. Indeed, this slavery is more complete than that which enslaves the body alone."

Henry David Thoreau,
journal, December 4, 1860

> Brethen, arise, arise! Strike for your lives and liberties. Now is the day and the hour . . . Rather die free men than live to be slaves . . . Let your motto be resistance! Resistance! RESISTANCE!
>
> The Reverend Henry Highland Garnet, former slave, delivering "An Address to the Slaves of the United States" in 1843

A Loyal Slave REVOLTS

As rain drenched his Louisiana plantation on the night of January 8, 1811, Manuel Andry slept soundly. Other slave owners had been known to sleep with one eye open. Andry, however, felt assured that *his* slaves were under his thumb.

Andry held more than eighty people as slaves, more than any other slaveholder in the French territory of Louisiana. Known for "being very severe to his negroes," Andry and his youngest son, Gilbert, ran a strict plantation. The black men, women, and children enslaved on his property knew they had to fully obey their masters; otherwise, they risked a dreaded whipping. In addition, Andry employed a trusted slave driver named Charles Deslondes. When Deslondes spoke, the black workers listened.

Outside on this stormy night, Deslondes was talking. And two dozen black men, armed with machetes and knives, were paying close attention. One of the men was an unassuming, twenty-five-year-old carpenter named Harry; the other was an African named Quamana, who had been captured and forcibly shipped to Louisiana a mere five years earlier.

Deslondes had a plan: March into the house and kill Manual and Gilbert Andry. Arm themselves with the Andrys' guns and ammunition. March south for thirty-six miles to New Orleans, recruiting other blacks for their "army" along the way. Overthrow the whites of New Orleans, like the enslaved on Haiti had overthrown their French masters a few years earlier, and seize state power throughout the New Orleans area—at the time home to about 25,000 people, 11,000 of whom were being held against their will as slaves.

It was an outlandishly ambitious plot, but, to these men, it was worth the attempt. What did they have to lose? For many of the men, death was more desirable than a lifetime of oppression, humiliation, and backbreaking work from dawn to dusk.

At some point, we might assume, Manuel Andry heard not just the pounding of raindrops on his roof but the stomping of many feet up the double staircase that led to the second floor, where he and his son slept. Andry awoke to the sight of Deslondes, his loyal assistant turned rebel, ordering his men to butcher the slave owner with an axe.

Frightened to flight, Andry bolted toward the door. Three blades sliced his body, and in a horrifying moment, he witnessed the killing of his son with another axe. But somehow, Andry was able to race down the stairs and, ironically, run to freedom and alert fellow planters to the "horde of brigands."

Andry and his son had been leaders of a colonial militia. As the freedom seekers gathered the guns and ammo that they found on the property, Deslondes and several others donned the Andrys' militia uniforms. After mounting a horse, Deslondes resembled a general of a revolutionary army.

Over the next two days, this band of self-emancipated slaves marched along River Road toward New Orleans, beating drums, waving flags, and reportedly chanting "Freedom or death" and "On to New Orleans." Accounts differ, but at least one hundred and perhaps as many as five hundred black men and women on other plantations joined their ranks. The makeshift but disciplined army came within

fifteen miles of New Orleans, and along the way they hacked to death at least two planters, burned five plantation houses (three to the ground) as well as several sugar houses and crops, and chased away dozens of whites and loyal slaves. Some historians have called it the largest uprising of enslaved people in American history.

Word of the revolt traveled faster than the freedom seekers could walk. Before they could reach New Orleans, three companies of federal troops and two companies of Louisiana militia, mounted on horses and accompanied by hunting dogs, engaged them in battle. The lightly armed blacks had no chance against the combined force of nearly seven hundred trained U.S. Army soldiers, militiamen, and slave owners, including Manuel Andry, who later described the rout as "*un grand carnage*" ("a great slaughter").

More than sixty black men were killed, and seventy-five were held for questioning and trials by parish courts—all French and comprised of plantation owners, some of whom had suffered property damage. Many of those captured were convicted and executed. Moreover, as a lesson to all enslaved men, women, and children living in the region, the heads of the executed were chopped off

The Destrehan Plantation, site of the trial and sentencing of the captured leaders of the 1811 Slave Revolt, also known as the German Coast Uprising. Destrehan was used as a location in the films *12 Years a Slave* (2013) and *Interview with the Vampire: The Vampire Chronicles* (1994).

A depiction of the enslavement of a white seaman by Africans

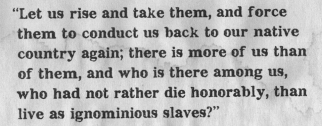

"Let us rise and take them, and force them to conduct us back to our native country again; there is more of us than of them, and who is there among us, who had not rather die honorably, than live as ignominious slaves?"

Blay, an enslaved African on an English vessel carrying him to the Americas.

Live Free
or DIE

rom the very dawn of the transatlantic slave trade, Africans resisted their capture and enslavement. They resisted in Africa, onboard slaving vessels, and in the New World.

The Atlantic slave trade dates back to 1441. At that time, Prince Henry of Portugal, known as Henry the Navigator, oversaw numerous seaward explorations. Henry was trying to find a water route to Asia, where coveted spices and silk were sold, and he wanted to continue to explore the coast of Africa, a land rich with spices, ivory, and gold.

That year, 1441, Henry authorized a journey to the West African coast led by Nuno Tristão and Antão Gonçalves. The navigators brought twelve Africans back to Portugal for their king. Over the next four centuries, many European countries engaged in the capture, purchase, and/or trading of millions of African people. In what was called the "Middle Passage," Europeans acquired people in Africa and forced them onto ships bound for the New World, where they were sold into slavery. The Europeans used that money to purchase such goods as tobacco, sugar, and coffee, which they took back to their home countries.

European slave traders were guilty of this horrible crime, but so too were the heads of African tribes and states. Many of them willingly and eagerly engaged in the slave-trading industry. They raided villages and kidnapped men, women, and children for the sole purpose of trading them to the Europeans for weapons, rum, cloth, and other goods. European powers were even known to encourage warfare within Africa in order to up the number of prisoners of war—that is, available slaves.

Splintered into thousands of tribes and states, Africa as a whole could not stop the barbarous practice of slave trading. But that did not stop individual tribal leaders and ordinary Africans from trying. Europeans were always looking over their shoulders, well aware that slave trading was a dirty business, rife with peril and danger.

In 1454, Italian slave trader and explorer Alvise Ca'Damosto and his party battled more than 150 fighting men on the River Gambia. Ca'Damosto learned through an interpreter why the men had fought so fiercely. "They firmly believed that we Christians ate human flesh," he wrote.

Three centuries later, another slaver plying the waters of the Gambia River met a similar fate. "[A sloop commanded by Captain Ingledieu, while] slaving up the River *Gambia,* was attacked by a number of Natives," according to a 1759 report in the *Gazette and Country Journal* of South Carolina, "the Captain finding himself desperately wounded, and likely to be overcome, rather than fall into the Hands of such merciless Wretches, when about 80 Negroes had boarded his Vessel, discharged a Pistol into his Magazine, and blew her up."

Along the West African coast, slave traders faced endless perils and confrontations. In 1704, three agents of the Royal African Company were stripped naked and held prisoner on the Senegambian coast. And in 1717, Captain David Francis reported, "my boats and people are seized at almost every port I send them."

King Trudo Audati, or Agaja, of Dahomey (in present-day Benin), who ruled from 1718 to 1740, regularly attacked the forts that the European powers had constructed on the coast. And more than a few African kings and rulers pleaded in letters to their counterparts in Europe to stop sending their merchants to kidnap and buy Africans. In 1526, King Nzinga Mbemba of the Kongo, then the largest state in central West Africa, wrote a letter to

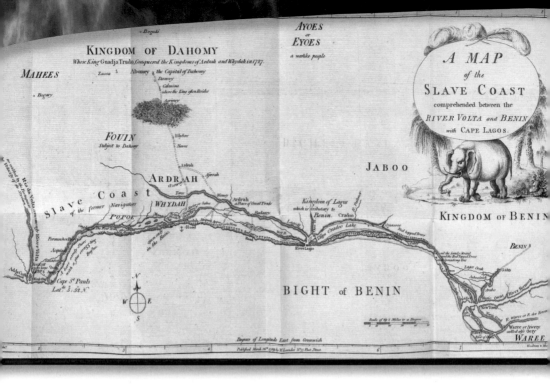

A 1789 map of the Kingdom of Dahomy, also spelled Dahomey

King Joao III of Portugal complaining of Portuguese traders kidnapping "our natives, sons of the land and the sons of our noblemen and vassals and our relatives. . . . So great, Sir, is the corruption and licentiousness that our country is being completely depopulated, and Your Highness should not agree with this nor accept it as in your service."

When verbal appeals failed, African rulers like Abdel Kader Kane, the Muslim leader of a region in northern Senegal, resorted to death threats. "We are warning you that all those who will come to our land to trade [in slaves] will be killed and massacred," Kane said in a letter to a French leader. "We absolutely do not want you to buy Muslims under any circumstances. . . . You should stay home and not come to our country anymore. Because all those who will come can be assured that they will lose their life."

Some African monarchs and rulers decided their only option against the raiding Europeans was to kill them. Military strategist Queen Nzinga Mbandi of the Ndongo and Matama kingdoms (in modern Angola) led her people in major revolts against the Portuguese for decades. She also offered sanctuary to runaway Africans and Portuguese-trained African soldiers; though, in the end, she was forced to compromise.

As word of the European kidnappers spread to African villages, many ordinary Africans simply packed up and fled. Whole villages relocated to regions further into the African interior, in hopes of safeguarding themselves and their loved ones. But the long reach of the trade eventually made its way deeper and deeper into the formerly uncharted terrain, finding them. No place was truly safe.

African-born Venture Smith wrote a memoir in which he told the story of his father's attempt to hide and protect his family and village, as well as protect a neighboring king and his people from invaders of "some white nation."

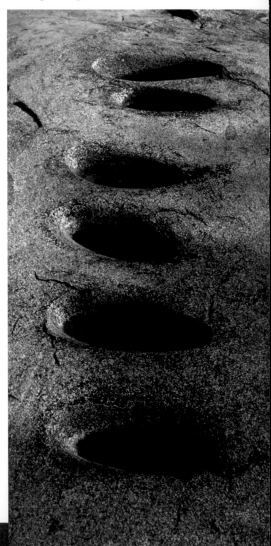

"Eating bowls" at Pikworo Slave Camp, in northern Ghana. The holes in the rock were dug out by the enslaved to use as bowls.

"The army of the enemy was large," Smith wrote. "I should suppose consisting of about six thousand men." He also recounted how his father defended himself and his people "with great firmness and courage, till at last he was obliged to surrender himself into their hands. . . . They then came to us in the reeds, and the very first salute I had from them was a violent blow on the head with the fore part of a gun, and at the same time a grasp round the neck. I then had a rope put about my neck."

After the kidnappers tortured his father to death, they marched Smith and the remaining captives toward the sea. "The enemy had remarkable success in destroying the country wherever they went. For as far as they had penetrated, they laid the habitations waste and captured the people. The distance they had now brought me was about four hundred miles. All the march I had very hard tasks imposed on me . . . being only about six years and a half old."

Slave Ship, a painting by William Jackson, on display at the National Maritime Museum in London

While at sea, Africans continued to fight against their enslavement. Some tried shaming slave ship captains and their crew into returning them to their native land. Synego, a kidnapped African speaking through an interpreter, gave this impassioned plea:

> You came to our country; you and your friends were treated with hospitality; we washed and anointed your feet; we gave you the best of our wines to drink, our most delicious food to eat; we entertained you with every amusement our country could afford. You invited us to see your ship . . . you traitorously gave us opiates, which caused us to sleep, you bound us captives and bore us away to this place; you . . . ravished our wives and daughters, whipped us with many stripes, starved our children to death, and suffered others to die unnoticed. And now you hold us in bondage and oblige us to work unceasingly. Is this the reward of friendship, hospitality and protection? Are you a christian people? If you are what you profess to be, a christian; repent and let us, whom you call heathens, return to our once happy shores.

Other Africans committed suicide by drowning, or by refusing to eat or to take medicine. One slave ship captain made it as far as the West Indies, only to have the Africans onboard his ship attempt suicide *en masse*. He reported, "thought all our troubles of this Voyage were over; but on the contrary . . . to our great Amazement about an hundred Men Slaves jump'd over board, and it was with great Difficulty we sav'd so many as we did. . . . Many more of them were taken up almost drown'd, some of them died since."

When all else failed, the Africans mutinied. In fact, shipboard rebellions were so frequent that ship owners routinely took out insurance to cover losses from mutinies. Historians have estimated that there was probably at least one insurrection every eight to ten journeys.

Not even a safe landing on the shores of the New World guaranteed that Africans would submit and accept their enslavement. An English traveler observed in 1746 that an African-born captive, "if he must be broke, either from Obstinacy, or, which I am apt to suppose, from Greatness of Soul, will require . . . hard Discipline . . . you would really be surpriz'd at their Perseverance; . . . they often die before they can be conquer'd."

Many Africans fled or attempted suicide as soon as their feet touched soil in the New World. That was the case in May 1803 when ten Nigerian men decided they would rather die than live as slaves. The ten were among seventy-five captured men, women, and children from a tribe called Igbo, or Ibo. When the schooner that carried them landed on a bluff in Georgia, an Igbo chief marched not to the shore but to his death in the creek, singing, "The water spirit Omambala brought us; the water spirit Omambala will take us away." At least nine other men followed, also singing.

Africans enslaved in the Caribbean, South America, and Mexico rebelled more often and in larger numbers than those in North America, especially in places where there was a high ratio of blacks to whites and slaves to free men, such as in Jamaica, Haiti, Brazil, and British Guyana. "Every part of the world where domestic slavery is established may be occasionally liable to insurrection and disquiet, more especially where the slaves constitute the majority of inhabitants," noted one slaveholder in his log. The first large-scale revolt of enslaved Africans took place on the sugar plantation of Christopher Columbus's son, Don Diego Colon, on December 25, 1522, four miles from Santo Domingo, on the island of Hispaniola. In 1546, Africans enslaved in Mexico revolted, as did those in Venezuela between 1552 and 1556.

Some of the bravest black captives of all were those who escaped from plantations and organized themselves into communities located in hard-to-reach places like mountains and swamplands. Known as maroons, these communities existed wherever slavery existed—from 1642 to 1864, they provided safe havens for fugitive slaves, served as bases for guerrilla attacks against nearby plantations, and, at times, supplied leadership for planned insurrections.

One of the earliest maroon communities formed in 1663 in Dutch and French Guyana, in South America. Planters sent some of their enslaved people into the forest to avoid paying taxes on them, and after the assessment was done, the enslaved refused to return.

Nanny of the Jamaican Maroons

The face on the five-hundred-dollar bill in Jamaica is that of an eighteenth century warrior named Queen Nanny or Granny Nanny. Described as the spiritual, cultural, and military leader of the Windward Maroons, this national heroine led many successful battles against the British. Located high in the Blue Mountains, on the east side of Jamaica, the Windward Maroons consisted of three hundred of the island's best fighting men. Their leader, Nanny, was described as ferocious by one British lieutenant, who reported to the Queen that "The old Hagg . . . had a girdle around her waste with nine or ten different knives hanging in sheaths to it, many of which I have no doubt, have been plunged in human flesh and blood." Legend has it that Nanny wore anklets made of the teeth of slain British soldiers. Novels, plays, songs, and poems celebrate Nanny and her exploits. Most of what is known about her comes from oral tradition; there are few written records to separate the truth and myth of her existence. Nevertheless, she remains an awe-inspiring symbol of unity and strength in Jamaica.

Until the mid-1700s, a large number of maroons lived downriver from New Orleans. In Florida, many Maroons aligned themselves with the Seminole Indians. And along the Virginia/North Carolina border, they lived along the Great Dismal Swamp.

Maroons focused on their own survival, which was difficult considering their meager resources. They not only had to struggle to produce food and shelter, but they had to fortify their communities against attack. In addition, some of these maroons engaged in guerrilla warfare against whites.

During the Revolutionary war about a hundred escaped slaves—who called themselves the "King of England's Soldiers"—waged attacks on plantations and state troops in Georgia. And in 1795, whites in North Carolina felt threatened by a maroon known as the "General of the Swamps." They formed special hunting parties and took him down, but maroon communities would continue to survive up to the Civil War.

Octave Johnson, a twenty-one-year-old runaway who joined a band of maroons outside New Orleans, described his life to a Union soldier during the Civil War:

Jamaican maroons fought against the British in the hills of this rainforest.

I had to steal my food; took turkeys, chickens, and pigs; before
I left our number had increased to thirty, of whom ten were
women; we were four miles behind the plantation house;
sometimes we would rope the beef cattle and drag them to
our hiding place; we obtained matches from our friends on the
plantation; we slept on logs and burned cypress leaves to make
a smoke and keep away mosquitoes; Eugene Jardeau, master
of hounds, hunted for us for three months; often those at work
would betray those in the swamp for fear of being implicated
in their escape; we furnished meat to our fellow-servants in
the field, who would return corn meal . . .

Whatever the method, enslaved Africans and their descendants found
varied and enterprising ways to exercise some measure of control over the
wretched, inhumane circumstances in which they found themselves. Though
largely powerless and downtrodden, they never stopped trying to shape their
own destinies and never gave up hope for a better day. As one enslaved man,
Lunsford Lane, put it, "I saw no prospect that my condition would ever be
changed. Yet I used to plan in my mind from day to day, and from night to
night, how I might be free."

An 1862 image taken in Beaufort, South Carolina, showing a group of Federals seated at a table with black servants standing around them.

"God's gonna set the world on fire,
one of these days . . ."

Negro Spiritual

"The Negros Are RISING!"

O ne of the first-documented, and largest, American rebellions staged
by enslaved Africans occurred three hundred years ago, and in the
unlikeliest of places: New York City. On New Year's Day, 1712, a group of
enslaved and free blacks gathered in New York City. Their mission: Destroy all
the whites in their path in order to gain their freedom.

To slave owners, free black people were a dangerous element. They
could supply their enslaved brethren with ammunition, information, and
transportation. In the south, there were few free blacks, so blacks forced to
work on southern plantations had little or no contact with them. But in the
north, in places like New York, enslaved and free black people interacted
frequently, and in this case, it led to the forming of a conspiracy.

The leaders of the plot, Akan people from the Gold Coast of West Africa,
claimed to practice magic. One gave his black comrades powder to rub on
their clothes—a substance, he claimed, that would make them invulnerable if
attacked by whites. To signify their commitment to the uprising, the plotters
tied "themselves to secrecy by Sucking ye blood of each Others hand."

At midnight on April 6 or 7, some two dozen of these freedom seekers gathered together. They began by setting fire to a building. When whites arrived, they attacked them with guns, swords, daggers, hatchets, clubs, and knives. They killed nine white men and seriously injured several others. It was one of the deadliest uprisings in the eighteenth century.

The plotters fled the scene, but soldiers and militiamen hunted them down. Within twenty-four hours, most were captured. Realizing the horrific fate that awaited them, six of the conspirators committed suicide. Wrote Reverend John Sharpe, chaplain of the English garrison in New York, one of the freedom seekers "shot first his wife and then himself" while others "cut their own throats."

Of the twenty-seven blacks captured, twenty-one were executed. Records state that some of them were hanged and others were burned alive. One died by "slow fire," so that he might "continue in torment for eight or ten hours." Another was broke on a wheel, meaning tied to a large wheel and abused until he died. Yet another was hung alive in chains for everyone in the area to see.

Aerial view of New York City

In the wake of the uprising, the New York Assembly passed an "Act for the suppressing and punishing the conspiracy and insurrection of Negroes and other Slaves." Blacks who were found guilty of murder, rape, arson, or assault were to "suffer the pains of death, in such manner and with such circumstances as the aggravation or enormity of their crimes . . . shall merit and require." The law also prohibited free blacks from owning property.

Throughout the slavery era, blacks who murdered whites were punished in the most barbaric fashion possible. Whites needed to make a statement that rebellion would not and could not be tolerated. Their society, and their own personal wealth and survival, depended on the complete suppression of the black people they held in bondage. Considering also that whites thought of blacks as less than human, it's not surprising that the punishment for these crimes was often worse than death.

Human oppression took a psychological toll not just on those enslaved but on slave-owning families. Many whites feared that they would be poisoned, shot to death, or have their throats slit. Southern women were known to sleep with a gun under their pillow. The most fearful and aggressive slave owners viciously whipped and beat the enslaved in an effort to ensure perpetual obedience.

Whites' fears of rebellion or "payback" were not unfounded. In 1751 in South Carolina, and 1770 in Georgia, legislatures established laws that called for the death of blacks who attempted to poison whites. Both laws were enacted in the wake of multiple poisoning attempts. The preamble of the South Carolina act stated, "the detestable crime of poisoning hath frequently been committed by slaves." Such laws, and the threat of death, meant little or nothing to some of the enslaved. One poisoner, described as "an old sullen house negress," regretted not putting enough arsenic in coffee to kill her tormentors. "I thought my master and mistress would get enough," the woman told a fellow bondswoman, "but it was not sufficient."

While slave owners could try to limit access to poison and weapons, they could not stop their black captives from creating fire. More often than poisoning, fed-up blacks vented their wrath through arson. Sarah, whom a Kentucky planter described as "the biggest devil that ever lived," poisoned "a stud horse and set a stable on fire, also burnt Gen. R. Williams stable and stock yard with seven horses and other property to the value of $1500. She was handcuffed and got away."

If slave owners lived in fear, they had only themselves to blame—or at least the system that their forefathers had created.

Slavery was by no means unique to America. Slavery had been commonplace in Europe, Asia, and Africa, and the practice of slavery dates back at least 5,000 years. Wrote David P. Forsythe: "at the beginning of the nineteenth century an estimated three-quarters of all people alive were trapped in bondage against their will either in some form of slavery or serfdom." Even today, upwards of 27 million people live in slavery, even though enslavement is illegal throughout the world.

In 1619, the Atlantic slave trade reached the current United States. Around that time, English colonists in Jamestown found great success growing tobacco, which they sold back to the home country. At first, their laborers came in the form of white indentured servants. Working-class Englishmen, who couldn't find work in their country, accepted passage to the British colonies in exchange for four to seven years of their labor.

While working for the plantation owners, these indentured servants received food, clothes, and shelter. After their period of indentured servitude was over, they received a large amount of land. The turnover rate of indentured servants was high, so planters looked for an alternative source of labor.

By happenstance, the first known African captives arrived in Jamestown. A Spanish slave ship, headed for one of Spain's colonies, was intercepted by a Dutch ship. The Dutch sailors

A *Harper's Weekly* illustration of the 1619 arrival of Africans at Jamestown stole the "human cargo." Afterward, this Dutch ship anchored at Jamestown. In need of supplies, the sailors traded twenty of the enslaved Africans for food.

Colonies and states created laws meant to strip the men and women they enslaved of freedom and keep them from rebelling. The South Carolina slave code of 1712, which would serve as a model for other colonies, forbade the enslaved from leaving their owners' property without permission, owning certain property, buying or selling goods, wearing clothes finer than "Negro cloth," and more. The acts of running away, burglary, arson, or assault of a white person could be punishable by death. Other laws prevented enslaved black people from gathering in groups, owning a weapon, or raising their hand to a white person, even in self-defense. Whites were committing a crime if they gave blacks alcohol or taught them to read or write. In short, every effort was made to keep the enslaved ignorant, docile, dependent, powerless, de-individualized, and, most of all, obedient.

On the plantations, where most powerless black men and women lived, conditions were bleak and frequently miserable. Black people were clothed and fed minimally, and most lived bunched together in wooden shacks with dirt floors. Children began running errands around age five, and by eight they would begin working on plantations. Fieldwork, which was physically taxing, lasted from morning to evening, even during blazingly hot summers in the Deep South.

Mississippi women
picking cotton

Often, a master would abruptly sell a parent, spouse, sibling, or child to another slave owner, permanently separating them from their loved ones. Besides the aforementioned capital-punishment crimes, blacks could be severely punished for seemingly minor infractions, such as not working hard enough, being disrespectful, insinuating threats, or talking in their native language. Whites punished blacks by whipping them, branding them with hot irons, chaining them, cutting off an ear, imprisoning them, forcing them to wear heavy metal collars, and killing them. In Arkansas, in 1853, a drunken overseer told an enslaved man named Nathan to take off his shirt so he could whip him. Fed up, a defiant Nathan told the overseer, "Shoot and be damned!" Three days later, Nathan died, of three gunshot wounds.

In 1740, South Carolina passed an anti-cruelty law that explained what whites could *not* do to blacks, such as burning, puncturing an eye, cutting out the tongue, and cutting off a limb. The fact that legislators had to specifically call these out implies that such barbaric punishment had already occurred.

Wilson Chinn was branded on his forehead with his owner's initials, "V. B. M." Chinn, age sixty in this 1864 photo, is wearing a contraption designed to prevent the enslaved from escaping. In the lower left corner is a paddle used to beat the enslaved.

Despite the threat of severe punishment for the slightest infractions, black people rebelled in a variety of ways. Mass revolt was relatively rare, but the rebellious act of running away was not. Lured by the dream of freedom, or simply unable to bear the ordeal of slavery anymore, thousands of black men, women, and children ran away. Considering that the South was a large landscape with virtually no safe havens for freedom seekers, and that they were hunted by men with guns and bloodhounds, many runaways faced a grim fate.

A slave ownership bracelet and key, circa 1746

Moses Grandy, who escaped from the South in 1833, described his fellow runaways:

> They hide themselves during the day in the woods and swamps; at night they travel, crossing rivers by swimming, or by boats they may chance to meet with, and passing over hills and meadows which they do not know; in these dangerous journeys, they are guided by the north-star, for they only know that the land of freedom is in the north. They subsist on such wild fruit as they can gather, and as they are often very long on their way, they reach the free states almost like skeletons.

Escaping on one's own was a near-impossible undertaking. However, from the early 1800s to the Civil War, the "Underground Railroad" helped tens of thousands of enslaved people escape to freedom in the North. *Railroad* was the figurative term for the escape network. It relied on funding from donors as well as the bravery of volunteers, who guided the enslaved northward.

Of course, anyone (black or white) who helped the enslaved escape would be severely punished if caught. In 1793, the U.S. Congress passed a law—signed by President George Washington—that would become known as the Fugitive Slave Act. The law required the return of escaped slaves to their owners even if they had fled their state.

"Freedom Suits"

In the state of Missouri alone, archivists sorting through millions of dusty, old court papers dating back to the Civil War have uncovered 301 "freedom suits" filed in St. Louis. The 301 cases were filed between 1814 and 1860, and about half of these St. Louis cases were successful.

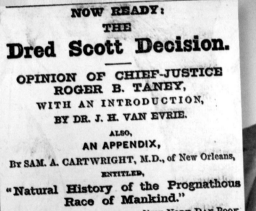

NOW READY:
THE
Dred Scott Decision.

OPINION OF CHIEF-JUSTICE ROGER B. TANEY,
WITH AN INTRODUCTION,
BY DR. J. H. VAN EVRIE.

ALSO,

AN APPENDIX,

By SAM. A. CARTWRIGHT, M.D., of New Orleans,

ENTITLED,

"Natural History of the Prognathous Race of Mankind."

ORIGINALLY WRITTEN FOR THE NEW YORK DAY-BOOK.

THE GREAT WANT OF A BRIEF PAMPHLET, containing the famous decision of Chief-Justice Taney, in the celebrated Dred Scott Case, has induced the Publishers of the DAY-BOOK to present this edition to the public. It contains a Historical Introduction by Dr. Van Evrie, author of "Negroes and Negro Slavery," and an Appendix by Dr. Cartwright, of New Orleans, in which the physical differences between the negro and the white races are forcibly presented. As a whole, this pamphlet gives the *historical, legal,* and *physical* aspects of the "Slavery" Question in a concise compass, and should be circulated by thousands before the next presidential election. All who desire to answer the arguments of the abolitionists should read it. In order to place it before the masses, and induce Democratic Clubs, Democratic Town Committees, and all interested in the cause, to order it for distribution, it has been put down at the following low rates, for which it will be sent, free of postage, to any part of the United States. Dealers supplied at the same rate.

Single Copies	$0 25
Five Copies	1 00
Twelve Copies	2 00
Fifty Copies	7 00
One Hundred Copies	12 00
Every additional Hundred	10 00

Address

VAN EVRIE, HORTON, & CO.,

An 1857 image of Dred Scott, and a clipping from *Century Magazine*

that freedom, which the great Parent of the Universe hath bestowed equally on all Mankind." Elizabeth Key Grinstead was the first enslaved woman to file a suit and win her freedom in the North American colonies. Elizabeth was born in 1630 to an enslaved black woman, but her white father owned the plantation where she lived. As an illegitimate child, she was expected to complete an indentured apprenticeship until age fifteen, when she would be free. However, when the plantation owner died, she was mistakenly classified in his estate as a slave. Elizabeth filed a "freedom suit" in 1655. She successfully argued that her English ancestry through her father prevented her from being enslaved for life.

The ultimate show of rebellion was all-out, armed revolt. Sometimes, a little flame of hope was enough to spark a revolt. Such was the case with the Stono Rebellion in the colony of South Carolina in 1739. In Europe that summer, Spain and England were on the verge of war. In America, Spaniards looked to cause unrest in the English Colonies by declaring that any enslaved person who deserted to St. Augustine, Florida (which was in Spanish territory), would be granted land and freedom.

Jemmy, an enslaved man born in the southern Africa country of Angola, planned a mass march to Florida. In the wee hours of September 9, about twenty other freedom seekers gathered near Stono River, less than twenty miles from Charlestown (now Charleston). Their first stop was a gun store, where they gathered firearms and ammunition and killed the two shopkeepers.

The self-emancipated slaves invaded homes and businesses with the purpose of killing whites. They entered the house of a Mr. Godfrey and murdered him and his son and daughter. Similar atrocities were committed at several other homes. Brazenly, the Africans marched down the road shouting "Liberty!" and carrying a banner that expressed that same word. By late afternoon, the band of freedom seekers—which had grown to approximately one hundred—had killed more than twenty whites.

Before dusk, dozens of armed whites arrived to shoot the rebels dead. They killed thirty of the men, and while many escaped, most were captured and executed before the month was over. With the exception of one, the rest were captured over the next six months.

The next year, South Carolina passed the Negro Act of 1740. The new law made it illegal for enslaved men and women to move abroad, assemble in groups, learn to read, earn money, or raise food. Moreover, slave owners were permitted to kill rebellious slaves.

The following year, in what became known as the New York Conspiracy, thirty black men were executed for allegedly setting thirteen fires in Lower Manhattan. One fire erupted in the lieutenant governor's mansion and spread to the secretary's office, where important documents were kept. At the time, New Yorkers worried about Spanish plans to gain control of North America. They also fretted about the growing number of enslaved black men in Manhattan, and feared a revolt.

As the fires raged in March and April, panic gripped the local population. At first, several "Spanish Negroes"—suspected of arson—were rounded up and jailed. Rumors began. Fingers were pointed. A conspiracy theory was formed: Blacks and poor whites had plotted to burn the city, kill the white men, and take control of government. "The Negroes are rising!" was chanted on the streets of New York.

Two black men were convicted and, as they were about to be burned at the stake, provided the names of "conspirators" in the hopes of preventing an agonizing death. Historians disagree about the existence of a conspiracy. However, in the minds of many law enforcement officials at the time, it had become cemented as fact. Some twenty whites and 150 blacks were arrested, and trials and executions took place throughout the summer. Seventeen black men were hanged, and thirteen were burned at the stake.

While the intentions of the Africans in New York were unclear, there's no denying the aims of certain Louisiana slaves in 1795. In what would be dubbed the Pointe Coupée Conspiracy, blacks intended to revolt on the night of April 12-13 on the estate of Julien Poydras, a poet, philanthropist, and slave owner. The time and place were ripe for a rebellion. Enslaved people outnumbered whites in the district 7,000 to 2,000, and the slave owners were isolated from each other.

The enslaved planned a spectacular rebellion. They would steal firearms and ammunition from Poydras and set one of his buildings ablaze. When whites came to extinguish the fire, they would gun them down. They would then march to other estates and murder the whites. While planning their uprising, leaders coordinated with blacks held on neighboring estates and even sympathetic whites, including a teacher named Josephy Bouyavel.

Just two days before the intended revolt, two Tunica Indian women betrayed the conspirators. They informed Spanish authorities (Louisiana was a Spanish territory at the time) that a rebellious plot was in the works. After getting confirmation of the rebellion from several witnesses, officers raided slave quarters, confiscated guns, and made dozens of arrests. Fifty-seven enslaved blacks and three whites were convicted of participating in the conspiracy.

Even though the blacks hadn't killed anyone, punishment was severe. Twenty-three people were executed, and their heads where nailed high on poles along the banks of the Mississippi River. With such gruesome images burned in their minds, the millions of black people held in perpetual bondage would think twice before fomenting another rebellion.

An 1895 map of Pointe Coupée Parish, Louisiana

"*Le Negre Marron*," often translated in English as the "Unknown Slave" statue, in Haiti. The *Negre Marron*, commissioned to commemorate enslaved people who revolted against France, has a machete in his right hand and his left hand holds a conch shell, which was often used as a trumpet to assemble people.

Liberte, Egalite, Fraternite,

the rallying cry of enslaved Africans on the island of Haiti, as they successfully fought to create the world's first black republic

The Fear of a Black Revolution

In the history of the Colonies and the United States, a large-scale, thousands-strong slave rebellion never materialized. However, whites always feared that such a massive revolt—or revolution—could come to fruition. They could point to Haiti and Jamaica as two examples.

During the French Revolution, the Declaration of Rights of Man was passed in France on August 26, 1789. It stated, "In the eyes of the law all citizens are equal." The French tried to keep word of this declaration from reaching its colonies, but it did reach the ears of black slaves in Haiti. Haitian slaves had been agitating for freedom for years, and after this ruling they insisted that they should be free.

The revolt began in Saint-Domingue, or Haiti, the source of roughly half of the world's coffee and sugar supplies. Some 40,000 whites lived nervously in Saint-Domingue, for they were outnumbered by some 480,000 blacks, close to 95 percent of whom were enslaved. A brewing storm of discontent evolved into an all-out revolt in August 1791. Enslaved men and women tortured, mutilated, and killed their white masters. During a period of weeks, upwards of 100,000 blacks joined the revolt, burning down close to two hundred sugar plantations and hundreds of coffee and indigo plantations.

An 1845 engraving of a scene from the Haitian Revolution. Toussaint L'Ouverture was the leader of the revolution. The French captured and deported him in 1802, but he declared, "In overthrowing me, you have done no more than cut down the trunk of the tree of black liberty in St. Domingue. It will spring back from the roots, for they are numerous and deep." One of his principal lieutenants, Jean Jacques Dessalines, led the Battle of Vertières, depicted here.

The Haitian Revolution lasted more than twelve years and resulted in the deaths of close to 200,000 people. In the end, the blacks prevailed. They formed the free republic of Haiti on January 1, 1804, and in subsequent months they carried out an ethnic cleansing, massacring the several thousand remaining whites on the island.

In the United States, news of the Haitian Revolution inspired many enslaved blacks and scared many whites, especially since the slave population in the U.S. was getting larger and larger—and, whites feared, more uncontrollable. From 1790 to 1830, the number of enslaved people rose from 700,000 to 2 million. The invention of the cotton gin, patented in 1794, was a key factor, for it revolutionized that industry. Cotton plantations, with blacks doing the bulk of the labor, dotted the southern landscape all the way to Texas.

Ironically, the slave population expanded despite the U.S. ban on the importation of slaves, which went into effect on January 1, 1808. That date had been decided upon by northern and southern negotiators at the

Constitutional Convention of 1787. They agreed that the practice would continue for twenty years after the adoption of the Constitution. After 1808, the number of slaves rose because of a high birthrate among enslaved women. As the number of enslaved blacks increased, so did the fear level of slaveholders.

If 100,000 Haitians could rise up and massacre their overseers, southern whites fretted, imagine the horrors of a million rebellious American slaves? In 1793, during the Haitian Revolution, U.S. president Thomas Jefferson echoed those fears: "It is high time we should foresee the bloody scenes which our children certainly, and possibly ourselves (south of [the Potomac River]) have to wade through, and try to avert them."

In 1831, southern whites received more frightening news from the Caribbean, this time from Jamaica. A British colony, Jamaica was home to some 300,000 enslaved people of African descent. Aware of the abolitionist movement underway in London, black Jamaicans advocated for their own freedom. Unlike in the U.S., black people in Jamaica were allowed to congregate for worship. Samuel Sharpe, a black Baptist preacher, took advantage of this opportunity. From his pulpit, he inspired his congregation and blacks in Jamaica to go on strike. They wanted more freedoms and to be paid for their labor.

After their demands were refused, the strike transformed into a massive rebellion. Upwards of 60,000 black Jamaicans ravaged more than two hundred plantations, and fourteen whites lost their lives. Unlike in Haiti, British forces easily suppressed the revolt. In addition to the two hundred or so enslaved who died during the rebellion, more than three hundred were executed.

Less than two years after this "Baptist War," the British Parliament passed the Slavery Abolition Act 1833, which abolished slavery throughout the British Empire. While an abolitionist movement was active in the northern United States, the southern states were completely committed to slavery; their economies depended on it.

Keeping millions of Africans and American-born blacks enslaved—and minimizing the threat of mass rebellion—was a difficult and sophisticated undertaking. It required not just brutal oppression but also religious propaganda and the inclusion of elasticity to the slavery system.

From the 1600s to the Civil War, southern legislatures passed hundreds of laws related to slavery. As discussed, enslaved people were not permitted to congregate, read, carry arms, etc. In the 1800s, states added many laws to the books to seal up any cracks— to make sure that black people had zero rights and that no one would dare to take part in an insurrection. In Virginia, an 1817 law stated that if a free person conspired with another free person to induce or excite a slave to rebel, the conspirator "shall be held a felon and suffer death by hanging." In 1839, Virginia declared it a felony for enslaved black men and women to cross ferries or bridges without their owners' written consent.

In 1829, the state of Georgia made it illegal to circulate printed material for the purposes of inciting blacks to insurrection. Beginning in 1833, white Georgians could be jailed if they were found teaching "any slave, negro, or free person of colour" to read or write. Two years later, Georgia prohibited enslaved and free black people from working in "Druggists and Apothecaries' stores." Other slaveholding states passed similar laws.

Of course, laws are only as strong as their enforcement. And in the South, there were plenty of enforcers, from paid officials to volunteer militias to the slaveholders themselves. Arnold Gragston of Kentucky said that his master, Mr. Tabb, "was a pretty good man." But if "we told him we had been learnin' to read, he would near beat the daylights out of us." Sara Benjamin, a slave in Louisiana, explained the consequences of literacy in her area: "If yer learned to write dey would cut yer thumb er finger off."

In the antebellum (pre-Civil War) South, cities and rural communities were heavily patrolled. Police, guards, soldiers, state militiamen, and volunteers on horseback were ever-present. Armed posses were always on the lookout for enslaved blacks who were in places they didn't belong, or who had gathered together. Frederick Law Olmsted, in his 1860 book *A Journey in the Back Country*, described the militaristic nature of Charleston, South Carolina:

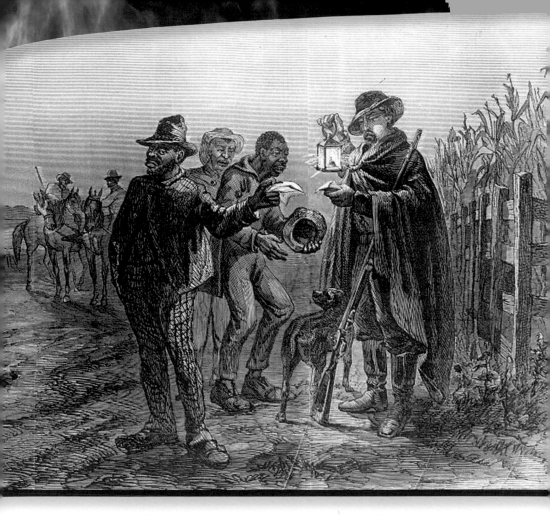

An 1863 illustration of plantation police checking the passes of the enslaved on the Levee Road below New Orleans

police machinery such as you never find in towns under free government: citadels, sentries, passports, grape-shotted cannon, and daily public whippings of the subjects for accidental infractions of police ceremonies. I happened myself to see more direct expression of tyranny in a single day and night in Charleston, than at Naples [Italy] in a week; and I found that more than half the inhabitants of this town were subject to arrest, imprisonment, and barbarous punishment, if found in the streets without a passport after the evening "gunfire." Similar precautions and similar customs may be discovered in every large town in the South.

Southern leaders realized that, in regards to the subjugation of black people, mind control could be as effective as military might. Politicians, clergymen, theologians, scientists, the press, and teachers perpetuated the myth that blacks were inferior beings and unworthy of equal status to whites. Some ministers preached that blacks descended from Cain, the "cursed" son of Adam and Eve; others claimed that the snake that had tempted Eve was really "the Negro." Even if they did not get that specific, clergymen insisted that slavery was God's will and need not be questioned.

In 1813, Reverend William Meade of the Virginia Episcopal Church authored *Sermons Addressed to Masters and Servants*. These sermons, which Episcopal ministers preached to their congregations, were aimed at the slaveholders and slaves, some of whom attended church with their masters on Sundays. Looking into the eyes of enslaved Africans, preachers insisted that they remain meek, humble, and obedient servants, else they be damned to Hell.

In this excerpt from one of Meade's sermons, blacks are told—through twisted logic—why it's best to accept punishment, such as whippings.

> Now, when correction [punishment] is given you, you either deserve it, or you do not deserve it. But, whether you really deserve it or not, it is your duty, and Almighty God requires, that you bear it patiently. . . . Or, suppose you are quite innocent of what is laid to your charge, and suffer wrongfully in that particular thing; is it not possible you may have done some other bad which was never discovered, and that Almighty God, who saw you doing it, would not let you escape without punishment, one time or another? And ought you not, in such a case . . . be thankful that he would rather punish you in this life for your wickedness, than destroy your souls for it in the next life? . . . [I]f you bear it patiently, and leave your cause in the hands of God, He will reward you for it in heaven, and the punishment you suffer unjustly here shall turn to your exceeding great glory hereafter.

Most of the enslaved saw through this propaganda. They didn't buy it. In what might be called spiritual rebellion, most black men and women believed in a different kind of God, in which the lowly would be rewarded in Heaven.

The slave system did include some elasticity. To remove *all* hope from slaves' lives would have caused most of them to just "give up," leading many to rebel (*What have I got to lose?*) or commit suicide (*What do I have to live for?*). Often, a hierarchy existed on plantations, which gave blacks hope for a better life. An obedient, hardworking person could rise from fieldworker to slave driver to domestic servant to personal servant.

Certainly, many fieldworkers—saddled with the burden of long, hard labor beneath the scorching heat of the sun—aspired for a promotion to domestic servant. Such servants, most of whom were women, cleaned, cooked, took care of children, and handled a variety of other chores.

Picking cotton is backbreaking work, and the echoes of the enslaved can be heard today in a slave-era song with these words: "*O Lord, O my Lord! O my good Lord keep me from sinking down.*"

What they didn't count on was rain. On Saturday, a torrential downpour flooded roads and washed out bridges. Gabriel postponed the revolt to the next evening, but by then it was too late. Two informants betrayed the plot to their masters, who alerted authorities. State militia and white patrols fanned across the state looking for rebels.

Realizing that their plan was doomed, Gabriel and many of his co-conspirators scattered in the countryside. By September 30, nearly thirty black rebels had been apprehended and sent to jail, where they awaited trial. Gabriel was one of them. Two weeks earlier, he had swum to a ship on the James River and asked to see the captain, Richardson Taylor. Though a former slave owner, Taylor agreed to take Gabriel to freedom. Ironically, an enslaved person on board the boat, Billy, betrayed the fugitive. Undoubtedly thinking of the three hundred dollar reward being offered for Gabriel's capture, Billy told authorities about him when the ship arrived in Norfolk. Billy received a reward, but it was only fifty dollars.

An illustration of Richmond, Virginia, in 1830

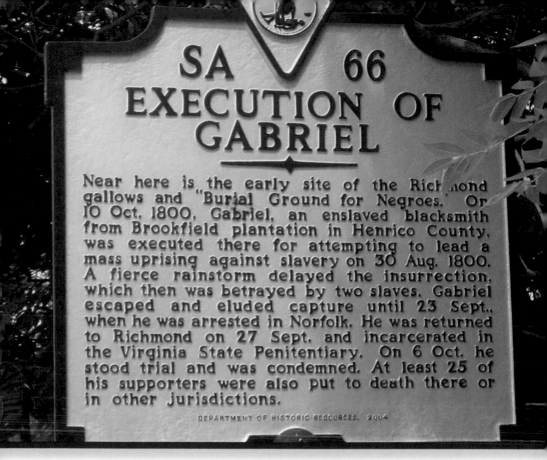

SA ∨ 66
EXECUTION OF GABRIEL

Near here is the early site of the Rich.nond gallows and "Burial Ground for Negroes." On 10 Oct. 1800, Gabriel, an enslaved blacksmith from Brookfield plantation in Henrico County, was executed there for attempting to lead a mass uprising against slavery on 30 Aug. 1800. A fierce rainstorm delayed the insurrection, which then was betrayed by two slaves. Gabriel escaped and eluded capture until 23 Sept., when he was arrested in Norfolk. He was returned to Richmond on 27 Sept. and incarcerated in the Virginia State Penitentiary. On 6 Oct. he stood trial and was condemned. At least 25 of his supporters were also put to death there or in other jurisdictions.

DEPARTMENT OF HISTORIC RESOURCES. 2004

Sign marker for Gabriel Prosser, who in 2010 received an informal pardon from Virginia governor Timothy M. Kaine. "Gabriel's cause—the end of slavery and the furtherance of equality of all people—has prevailed in the light of history," said Kaine.

On October 6, Gabriel went on trial. Found guilty, he was sentenced to be hanged the next day. The court granted Gabriel's wish to postpone the execution to October 10, so that he could be executed alongside six other condemned comrades. All were hanged on that day, but in a final indignity, Gabriel was hanged alone in a different location: the town gallows.

At the Richmond trial, one of the rebel defendants said of his own defense,

I have nothing more to offer than what General Washington would have had to offer, had he been taken by the British and put to trial by them. I have adventured my life in endeavouring to obtain the liberty of my countrymen, and am willing to sacrifice to their cause: and I beg, as a favour, that I may be immediately led to execution. I know that you have pre-determined to shed my blood, why then all this mockery of a trial?

All told, dozens of black rebels stood trial. A few were pardoned after giving testimony that doomed other conspirators. Many defendants were found not guilty or transferred to other states. More than two dozen were hanged.

Fearing future uprisings such as Gabriel's, Virginia Assembly members banned the hiring out of enslaved servants, believing that such freedom of movement contributed to rebellious plots. Moreover, freed blacks were required to leave the state within twelve months after obtaining their liberty.

The abolitionist movement wouldn't catch fire until the 1830s, but even before then many whites railed against slavery. George Boxley was one such man. He took the highly unusual path of slave owner to abolitionist to revolt leader to fugitive.

The owner of a general store in Spotsylvania, Virginia, Boxley kept three black people as slaves in 1815, the year of his planned revolt. A tall, light-haired man with large whiskers, the thirty-something Boxley believed in equality for all. He was said to have declared "that the distinction between the rich and the poor was too great; that offices were given rather to wealth than to merit," and he wished blacks were free.

After failing in his run for the state legislature, Boxley took extreme measures. In 1815, he conspired to free people enslaved on plantations in Spotsylvania, Louisa, and Orange counties. Fellow conspirators gathered swords, clubs, and guns. On one day in early 1816, they were to gather at Boxley's house with weapons and horses, attack the town of Fredericksburg, and then move on to the state capital of Richmond.

But as with Gabriel's revolt, an informant betrayed the plot—specifically, a black woman in Spotsylvania. Officials quickly arrested thirty blacks. After a failed attempt to organize a rescue party, Boxley fled. He eventually was captured, but he escaped from jail with the help of a small tool, smuggled to him by his wife.

Boxley and his family eventually settled in rural Indiana, where they reportedly contributed to the Underground Railroad by hiding escaping black men, women, and children beneath his cabin. Some of the black people who had conspired with him in Virginia were not so fortunate. Several were executed by hanging.

Denmark Vesey, a free black man, plotted his revolt in Charleston, South Carolina, a city with a history of uprisings and brutal suppression. Born around 1767, Vesey worked as a slave until 1799, when he purchased his freedom for six hundred dollars after winning $1,500 in a city lottery. It was a bittersweet experience for Vesey, whose wife and children remained enslaved. Somehow, someway, Denmark sought to bring down the whole system of slavery.

The bearded Vesey, who spoke several languages, earned a living as a carpenter. He joined the African Methodist Episcopal Church in 1817 and emerged as a leader, preaching to his followers in his home. Whites in Charleston monitored the church, arrested members, and shut it down twice—in 1818 and 1820. Their oppression fueled the ire of Vesey, who preached that the enslaved were the New Israelites.

In 1822, Vesey and his African Church comrades began to plot a revolt. Gullah Jack, a priest from Angola, was key to the campaign. Jack recruited many blacks to the cause, and he provided them with amulets, or charms, that he said would protect them from their white enemies.

The Vesey rebellion was based more on ideology than most other revolts. Besides the religious overtones, Vesey and his co-conspirators preached about the Haitian Revolution and read antislavery speeches related to the Missouri controversy. (In 1820, after much rancor, Missouri was admitted as a slaveholding state and Maine as a free state.) Said one rebel about Vesey: "He was in the habit of reading to me all the passages in the newspapers that related to St. Domingo, and apparently every pamphlet he could lay his hands on that had any connection with slavery."

Vesey and the rebels set July 14, 1822, as the day they would seize Charleston's arsenals and guard houses and murder the governor. They would set fire to the city, kill every white man they could, and then escape to Haiti. But as with other major slave rebellions, slaves betrayed the plot to their masters before it could materialize. The word got out as early as June, and Charleston officials began arresting conspirators.

In total, Charleston authorities arrested more than 130 men, including the leader. While in confinement, Vesey told his doomed comrades, "Die like a man!" The conspirators, despite being tortured, refused to give up the names of their followers. Sixty-seven men were convicted, and thirty-five died by hanging, including Vesey on July 2.

AN

OFFICIAL REPORT

OF THE

TRIALS OF SUNDRY NEGROES,

CHARGED

WITH AN ATTEMPT TO RAISE

AN INSURRECTION

IN THE STATE OF SOUTH-CAROLINA:

PRECEDED BY AN

INTRODUCTION AND NARRATIVE;

AND

IN AN APPENDIX,

A REPORT OF THE TRIALS OF

FOUR WHITE PERSONS,

ON INDICTMENTS FOR ATTEMPTING TO EXCITE THE SLAVES TO
INSURRECTION.

Prepared and Published at the request of the Court.

⸺⸺

By LIONEL H. KENNEDY & THOMAS PARKER,
Members of the Charleston Bar, and the Presiding Magistrates of the Court.

⸺⸺

CHARLESTON:
PRINTED BY JAMES R. SCHENCK, 23, BROAD-STREET.

1822.

Besides burning down the African Church, city officials passed new laws that further restricted the rights of slaves and free blacks. To prevent foreigners of African descent from agitating enslaved blacks in Charleston, a new law compelled the forced imprisonment of black sailors visiting Charleston. A federal court would find this law to be unconstitutional. As for Vesey, his efforts were not in vain. He became a heroic martyr figure for blacks and a symbol for the abolitionist movement.

In 1831, another great slave insurrection began to brew, this time in Virginia. White Southerners could point the finger of blame at Benjamin Turner, the relatively lenient master of a black man named Nat. On Turner's plantation in Southampton County, Nat Turner was allowed to be instructed in reading, writing, and religion. Armed with such knowledge, Nat would foment a race war that would result in more than one hundred deaths.

Nat Turner was born in 1800, just days before Gabriel Prosser was hanged. His mother, an African native, relayed her intense hatred of slavery to her son. Nat, who learned to read from one of his master's sons, was keenly intelligent and deeply devoted to his religion. In fact, he became somewhat of a hermit. He prayed, fasted, and avoided social interaction. Fellow blacks viewed this religious, mysterious man as a prophet, destined for great things.

In 1821, Nat ran away, but after being gone for a month he stunningly came back. He explained that he had had a vision in which the spirit told him to "return to the service of my earthly master." When that master died, a year later, Nat was sold to a nearby farmer named Thomas Moore. In 1824, Nat had another vision: "I then found on the leaves in the woods hieroglyphic characters and numbers, with the forms of men in different attitudes, portrayed in blood."

Nat's third vision, on May 12, 1828, was much more alarming:

I heard a loud noise in the heavens, and the Spirit instantly appeared to me and said the Serpent was loosened, and Christ had laid down the yoke he had borne for the sins of men, and that I should take it on and fight against the Serpent, for the time was fast approaching, when the first should be last and the last should be first. . . . And by signs in the heavens that it would make known to me when I should commence the great work—and until the first sign appeared, I should conceal it from the knowledge of men—And on the appearance of the sign . . . I should arise and prepare myself, and slay my enemies with their own weapons.

By 1831, Thomas Moore had died and his wife had married Joseph Travis. Nat considered Travis a kind master and was not upset with how Travis treated him. In February, Nat witnessed an eclipse of the sun, which he interpreted as his call for action. After conferring with his four trusted friends—Henry, Hark, Nelson, and Sam—Nat planned his "work of death" for the Fourth of July. But the stress of the undertaking caused Nat to fall ill, prompting them to delay their plans.

On August 21, Nat and his friends met in the woods and, while dining on pork and brandy, concocted their insurrection. The first to die would be Joseph Travis and his family. That night, while Travis and his wife and children lay sleeping, the small band of rebels went to their house. Hark planned to bust open the door with an axe, but that would have caused alarm in the neighborhood. So, Nat said, "we determined to enter the house secretly, and murder them whilst sleeping."

Nat ascended a ladder, entered a window, grabbed some guns, and opened the door for his comrades. In *The Confessions of Nat Turner*, published by a local lawyer later that year, Nat explains what happened next in chilling detail:

An 1880 illustration of Nat Turner and his followers gathering to plan a revolt

It was then observed that I must spill the first blood. On which armed with a hatchet, and accompanied by Will, I entered my master's chamber; it being dark, I could not give a death blow, the hatchet glanced from his head, he sprang from the bed and called his wife, it was his last word. Will laid him dead, with a blow of his axe, and Mrs. Travis shared the same fate, as she lay in bed. The murder of this family five in number, was the work of a moment, not one of them awoke; there was a little infant sleeping in a cradle, that was forgotten, until we had left the house and gone some distance, when Henry and Will returned and killed it. . .

Emboldened by the murders, Nat formed the rebels in a line, as if they were soldiers, and marched them to the home of Salthul Francis. They killed Francis with blows to the head, then marched quietly to Mrs. Reese's house, where they killed the woman while she slept. Her son awoke, but, Nat recalled, "he had only time to say who is that, and he was no more."

By sunrise on Monday, the band reached the home of Mrs. Turner, the wife of Nat's former owner. Realizing they were under siege, the family shut the door. "Vain hope!" Nat wrote. "Will, with one stroke of his axe opened it, and we entered and found Mrs. Turner and Mrs. Newsome in the middle of a room, almost frightened to death. Will immediately killed Mrs. Turner, with one blow of his axe." Since Nat had a hard time killing Mrs. Newsome with his dull sword, Will finished her off.

By this time, Nat's army had grown to two dozen men. After each murder, they destroyed property and searched for money and ammunition. Their party grew, and the killing rampage became even more heinous. On the Whitehead property, Will killed Richard Whitehead with an axe in a cotton patch before nearly decapitating Mrs. Whitehead with a powerful chop. As a Miss Margaret tried to flee, Nat delivered a fatal blow to her head with a fence rail.

Nat said that his objective was "to carry terror and devastation wherever we went." He said he viewed mangled bodies "in silent satisfaction, and immediately started in quest of other victims." Almost casually, Nat mentioned that they "murdered Mrs. Waller and ten children," and then afterward killed William Williams and two small boys. Mrs. William fled, but a rebel brought her back to the house. "After showing her the mangled body of her lifeless husband," Nat recalled, "she was told to get down and lay by his side, where she was shot dead."

At midday on the 22nd, with Nat's army having grown to more than fifty men, they encountered a militia. After gunfire was exchanged, Nat ordered his troops to rush the armed whites. But the militia was too strong, and the rebels retreated and dispersed. This ended their killing spree, which had amounted to sixty dead white men, women, and children. Nat and two comrades, Jacob and another Nat, hid together in the woods, but soon Nat Turner was all alone. He hid in several places for weeks until his capture on October 30.

Nat delivered his confession to Thomas R. Gray, a Southampton County attorney, while in jail. On November 5, he was sentenced to execution, and six days later he died by hanging. His body was skinned, beheaded, and quartered.

Nat was one of more than fifty rebels whom the state executed, and that wasn't all. The gruesome killings sparked fear and vengeance among white communities, leading to mob violence. In the aftermath of the revolt, approximately two hundred black people were killed.

Not surprisingly, laws related to slavery and free blacks became even stricter in the Nat Turner aftermath. In Virginia itself, the General Assembly passed multiple laws shortly after the rebellion. Those of African descent were no longer allowed to preach at religious meetings. Any enslaved or free black who held a religious meeting would be sentenced to a public whipping of thirty-nine lashes. Any enslaved person who even attended a religious gathering could be subjected to a public whipping.

The General Assembly ruled that if an enslaved person or free black wrote or printed something that advised blacks to commit insurrection, to riot, or to assemble unlawfully, that person would be whipped. The legislature also prohibited blacks from distributing liquor near any public assembly. Moreover, the rights of free blacks to own slaves were curtailed.

In the wake of the Nat Turner Revolt, some whites in Virginia wanted to be done with slavery. The large numbers of blacks in the state made many people nervous. Also, with a shift away from tobacco, the state no longer needed as many enslaved people. The increasingly popular practice of hiring out the enslaved—like Nat's master had done with him—was considered dangerous, for it meant less control of the black people they kept as slaves. Others worried about the mixing of races (even former Virginia governor Thomas Jefferson was rumored to have fathered children with one of his black servants, Sally Hemings).

As it turned out, many enslaved blacks in the Upper South were sold to Deep South slave owners in the early to mid-1800s, mainly because of the booming cotton industry. Overall, slavery after Nat Turner did not diminish in the U.S. but instead expanded. From 1830 to 1860, the number of enslaved people in the South grew from 2 million to 4 million.

Did he? Or, didn't he?

The question of whether Thomas Jefferson fathered children with a woman he kept as a slave has festered in the minds of many for generations. And perhaps we'll never know the truth. However, according to the "Report of the Research Committee on Thomas Jefferson and Sally Hemings," which was commissioned by the Thomas Jefferson Foundation, "Thomas Jefferson was the father of the six children of Sally Hemings mentioned in Jefferson's records, including Beverly, Harriet, Madison, and Eston Hemings." (Only four of the six children survived till adulthood.) This conclusion is based on documentary, statistical, scientific, including DNA testing, and oral history evidence.

Thomas Jefferson at Mount Rushmore National Memorial

"*Porquoi! Naitre esclave* (Why born a slave?)." This is the inscription on the base of *La Négresse*, a bust created by Frenchman Jean-Baptiste Carpeaux in 1868. The plaster bust featured here is patterned after Carpeaux's bronze, which is on display at the Indianapolis Museum of Art. A terracotta copy is also on display at the Metropolitan Museum of Art of New York City.

CHAPTER 5

"I had reasoned dis out in my mind; there was one of two things I had a right to, liberty, or death; if I could not have one, I would have de oder; for no man should take me alive; I should fight for my liberty as long as my strength lasted . . ."

Harriet Tubman, former slave, Underground Railroad leader, Civil War spy and general for the Union Army

The Peculiar Burdens of Enslaved Women

Harriet Ann Jacobs was born into slavery in 1813 and grew up in Edenton, North Carolina. Until the age of six, Harriet enjoyed a normal, happy life—*that is* as much as a person in bondage can enjoy a normal life. "Though we were all slaves, I was so fondly shielded that I never dreamed I was a piece of merchandise," Jacobs recalled in an autobiography called *Incidents in the Life of a Slave Girl*.

Jacobs's mother died when she was six, and the woman who owned her mother died when the girl was twelve. Ownership of Jacobs then transferred to the woman's niece. But since the niece was only three years old, Harriet's actual master was the father, a Dr. James Norcom, a man who would pursue her with a vengeance.

Dr. Norcom was relentless in his sexual advances toward and harassment of Jacobs. "I now entered on my fifteenth year. . . . He peopled my young mind with unclean images, such as only a vile monster could think of. I turned from him with disgust and hatred. But he was my master. I was compelled to live under the same roof with him—where I saw a man forty years my senior daily violating the most sacred commandments of nature."

From 1825 to 1842, the year Harriet escaped to freedom in Philadelphia, Jacobs was terrorized by Norcom, whose sexual quest to have her—even after she gave birth to a son and daughter by another man—knew no bounds.

Harriet Jacobs

He told me I was his property; that I must be subject to his will in all things. My soul revolted against the mean tyranny. But where could I turn for protection? . . . My master met me at every turn, reminding me that I belonged to him, and swearing by heaven and earth that he would compel me to submit to him. If I went out for a breath of fresh air, after a day of unwearied toil, his footsteps dogged me. If I knelt by my mother's grave, his dark shadow fell on me even there.

"Slavery is terrible for men," Jacobs wrote, "but it is far more terrible for women. Superadded to the burden common to all, *they* have wrongs, and sufferings, and mortifications peculiarly their own."

Jacobs was one of millions to suffer the unique double-burden of being enslaved and a woman, in the white male-dominated business of slavery. Historians are rarely able to agree on the number of people forcibly shipped from Africa to the New World during the four-hundred-year span of the Atlantic slave trade. The number is put at somewhere between nine and sixteen million. However, nearly all seem to agree that one-third of the people shipped across the Atlantic were women, meaning three to five million landed in the New World. Whatever the actual number, it is clear that black women were no more willing to accept life as a slave than men.

In many ways, enslaved women were treated no differently than enslaved men. Both sexes were considered beasts of burden, "chattel." Enslaved women worked as hard as enslaved men, often for more years than men, because they lived longer. The majority performed agricultural work, such as clearing new land, building fences, hoeing fields, weeding and picking worms off plants, and planting and harvesting rice, sugar, tobacco, cotton, or corn. And, like men, they suffered lashings and beatings, if the sowing and harvesting were not fast enough or considered satisfactory. They also worked as washerwomen, water carriers, cooks, maids, cleaners, seamstresses, and wet nurses (breastfeeding the children of the slave master). When the South began to industrialize, women began working twelve to sixteen hours a day in coal mines, iron foundries, and at salt works, as well as in other heavy industry, such as ditch digging, rice milling, tobacco processing, lumberjacking, and sugar refining. In Louisiana, enslaved black women helped build levees and lay railroad tracks for southern railroads, and 50 percent of the workers who dug out the North Carolina Santee Canal were enslaved women.

In other ways, enslaved women, by virtue of their gender, experienced "mortifications peculiarly their own," as Harriet Jacobs put it. Because slave owners had no regard for the dignity of black women and considered them property, they believed they had the right to rape and sexually abuse them. Moreover, black women were considered "breeders," "producers." And, once women gave birth they were helpless as mothers to protect their children. "I was worth a heap to Marse George 'cause I had so many chillen," former slave Tempie Durnham recalled. "De more chillen a slave had de more dey was worth." Another former slave from Texas, Katie Darling, reported, "massa pick out a p'otly man and a p'otly gal and just put 'em together, What he want am the stock." Caroline Hunter, a slave from Portsmouth, Virginia, lamented, "During slavery it seemed lak yo' chillun b'long to ev'ybody but you."

All the Pretty Little Horses

Hushaby, don't you cry.
Go to sleep, little baby.
When you wake, you shall have cake.
And all the pretty little horses.
Blacks and bays, dapples and grays,
Coach and six-a little horses.

Way down yonder in the meadow.
There's a poor little lambie;
The bees and the butterflies
pickin' out his eyes.
The poor little thing cries.
"Mammy."

Hushaby, don't you cry.
Go to sleepy, little baby.

"All the Pretty Little Horses" is believed to be an authentic, slave-era lullaby. The lyrics expose the cruel irony and bitter feelings of an enslaved woman who sings to her master's child, promising cake and horses when the baby wakes, while mournfully acknowledging her own neglected baby, crying in a meadow.

Live oaks, fringed with Spanish moss, dominate the background of this photo of two little black girls holding the bars of a gate leading to an old rice planting plantation in an area known as Goose Creek, near Charleston, South Carolina.

Truth is, and historical records show, it was nearly impossible for the millions of African men, women, and children enslaved in the New World to do little more than accept their bondage. They arrived naked and chained in foreign lands, speaking hundreds of different languages, and with no possible means of getting back to their families and countries. Even in places where blacks outnumbered whites, whites not only had the guns and ammunition to quickly put down a rebellion, they held all power in their hands, having created a well-developed system of laws and judgments to keep blacks in a perpetual state of servitude. Nevertheless, in spite of the peculiar vulnerabilities and dangers they faced, enslaved women, like their male counterparts, found ways to rebel, fight back, and in some way or another, keep their hopes focused on a better day.

In places like the West Indies, it was not uncommon for women to lead uprisings and rebellions. A Yoruba woman named Carlota took up the machete in 1843 and, with two other enslaved comrades, led an uprising against the Spanish at the sugar estate Triumvirato in Cuba. She was captured, tortured, and killed. Today a monument at the Triumvirato Sugar Mill commemorates "Carlota's Rebellion."

Nanny Griggs of the Barbados helped plan a rebellion against British sugar planters on April 14, 1816, telling her followers that the only way to obtain freedom was to fight for it. And Cécile Fatiman, a Vodoo priestess, is credited with playing a key role in sparking the 1791 revolution against slavery in Haiti.

A statue commemorating Solitude, a historical figure in the fight against slavery on the French West Indies island of Guadeloupe. In May 1802, Solitude was taken prisoner by the French during a battle. Because she was pregnant, she was not hanged until November 29 of the same year, one day after giving birth.

In the American colonies, acts of resistance by enslaved women were more individual than collective. For example, years of pent-up anger and hostility seized Mary Armstrong one day, and she attacked her mistress, Miss Polly. "One day old Polly devil comes . . . and tries to give me a lick out in the yard, and I picks up a rock 'bout as big as half your fist and hits her right in the eye and busted the eyeball, and tells her that's for whippin' my baby sister to death." Celia, an enslaved woman in Missouri, killed her master in 1855, after repeatedly being raped by him and giving birth to several of his children as a result. To hide the crime, she cut her rapist into pieces and burned the body in a fireplace. Another black woman, who was beaten "near 'bout to death" by the overseer of the plantation, decided to meet evil with evil. She threw the overseer's child "in a pot of lye dat she was usin' to wash wid." The child's mother came out screaming and tried to rescue her child, "but it didn't do no good 'caze when she jerked de chile out he was daid."

Violence was not the only, or the most common, way that enslaved black women found ways to resist. Elizabeth Key Grinstead, who was born in 1630, sued for her freedom and won. So did Mum Bett, who sued her slave owner and won her freedom—plus back wages—in 1781. Ona Judge Staines, an enslaved women belonging to George Washington, ran away. During the fall of 1796, she made her way to Portsmouth, New Hampshire. The president tried his best to get her back, penning several correspondences and soliciting help from friends and family, but Staines eluded re-enslavement and settled in Greenland, New Hampshire. Ellen Craft, so light in complexion she could pass for white, disguised herself as a white southern planter and escaped to freedom in Philadelphia in 1848, with her husband, William, traveling as her slave. The "planter" and "his" slave traveled in first-class trains, dined with a steamboat captain, and stayed in top hotels during their escape. Mary Walker also fled to Philadelphia, in August of 1848. Born in 1818, she grew up on one of the largest and wealthiest plantations in North Carolina. After passage of the Fugitive Slave Act of 1850, abolitionists helped her escape a second time, to Massachusetts, where she spent the next seventeen years trying to free her children and reunite her family. Walker later owned 54 (now 56) Brattle Street, located in the heart of Harvard Square and today home to the Cambridge Center for Adult Education.

Enslaved women were required to wear head wraps or scarfs by their masters. What was meant as a badge of enslavement, however, became a form of cultural resistance and personal and communal identity. Nancy Burns, the woman in this 1844 portrait by Ferdinand Thomas Lee Boyd, was born into slavery but eventually obtained her freedom from a prominent New York family. Her portrait and simple, plaid scarf are on display at the American Museum in Britain.

Harriet Tubman and Sojourner Truth are perhaps the best known black women strategists against slavery, and the two deservedly receive credit in history books for their acts of defiance. However, the efforts of most enslaved black women were private, protracted, and heart-wrenching. Open acts of defiance were simply not an option for millions. Instead, quiet acts of persistence and resistance prevailed, and even then, any real or perceived resistance was dealt with harshly. Adeline Cunningham, for example, persisted in finding secret places to pray. "We never goes to church. Times we sneaks in de woods and prays de Lawd to make us free . . . dey heered at de big house and den de overseer come and whip us 'cause we prayed de Lawd to set us free."

Elizabeth Hobbs Keckley, born into slavery in Dinwiddie County, Virginia, in 1818, purchased her freedom in 1855. A favorite dressmaker of Mary Todd Lincoln, she became Mary Lincoln's personal companion, confidante, and traveling companion, until the 1868 publication of Keckley's autobiography, *Behind the Scenes, Or, Thirty Years a Slave and Four Years in the White House.* In an excerpt from her book, Keckley remembers a particular moment of strength:

I was thunderstruck, and tried to think if I had been remiss in anything. I could not recollect of doing anything to deserve punishment, and with surprise exclaimed: "Whip me, Mr. Bingham! What for?"

"No matter," he replied, "I am going to whip you, so take down your dress this instant."

Recollect, I was eighteen years of age, was a woman fully developed, and yet this man cooly bade me take down my dress. I drew myself up proudly, firmly, and said: "No, Mr. Bingham, I shall not take down my dress before you. Moreover, you shall not whip me unless you prove the stronger. Nobody has a right to whip me . . . and nobody shall do so if I can prevent it."

Elizabeth Hobbs Keckley

One of the most desperate forms of sabotage by enslaved women was taking poison to induce abortions or killing their children to save them from a life of slavery and abuse. According to the mistress of one plantation, an elderly cook named Sylva had "been the mother of thirteen children, every one of whom she has destroyed with her own hands in their infancy, rather than have them suffer slavery!"

Beloved

The inspiration for Nobel Prize-winning author Toni Morrison's novel, *Beloved*, was the real-life story of an enslaved woman named Margaret Garner. Garner was a runaway from Kentucky. Pregnant and twenty-two years old at the time of her escape, Garner fled with her husband, his parents, and her four children, in record cold temperatures. They crossed the frozen Ohio River into Cincinnati, but slave catchers and U.S. marshals soon caught up with them. Refusing to have her children taken back into slavery, Garner slit the throat of her baby daughter with a butcher knife. She wounded the other children in an attempt to kill them, and she planned to kill herself, but her captors subdued her before she could end more life.

The Modern Medea, an 1867 painting by Thomas Satterwhite Noble, based on Margaret Garner's story

White Women Abolitionists

Sarah Grimke (born 1792) and her sister Angelina, daughters of a slaveholding judge from South Carolina, hated slavery. After moving to Philadelphia in 1819, they joined the Quakers and produced some of the most powerful and influential antislavery publications in the antebellum era. Harriet Beecher Stowe wrote a novel, *Uncle Tom's Cabin*, based on Josiah Henson, an escaped slave whose narrative Stowe had read. Published in 1851, Stowe stated, "The object of these sketches is to awaken sympathy and feeling for the African race, as they exist among us; to show their wrongs and sorrows, under a system so necessarily cruel and unjust as to defeat and do away with the good effects of all that can be attempted for them by their best friends."

Sarah Grimke

The novel's first edition of 5,000 copies sold out in a week. Despite being banned in the South, more than 300,000 copies were sold in its first year. Frederick Douglass later pointed out: "Its effect was amazing, instantaneous and universal." Fanny Wright, a Scottish-born freethinker, purchased 2,000 acres of woodland near Memphis, Tennessee, in 1825 and formed a commune called Nashoba. Then she proceeded to buy enslaved people from neighboring farmers, free them, and give them land on her settlement. Three years later the Nashoba settlement failed, but Wright sent the former slaves to Haiti.

Josiah Henson

Vintage letterpress printing blocks

"O, that I were free! . . . O, why was I born a man, of whom to make a brute! I am left in the hottest hell of unending slavery. O, God, save me! God deliver me! Let me be free! Is there any God? Why am I a slave? I will run away. I will not stand it. Get caught, or get clear, I'll try it. . . . I have only one life to lose. I had as well be killed running as die standing."

Frederick Douglass

REBELLING
Through Words
and Deeds

When Americans fought for their freedom against the British in the 1770s, a cloud of hypocrisy hung over the Colonies. The Colonists felt oppressed by the taxes that the British levied against them. Claiming that the British Parliament had no right to exert its authority over the Colonies, Founding Father Patrick Henry exclaimed in 1775: "Is life so dear, or peace so sweet, as to be purchased at the price of chains and slavery? Forbid it, Almighty God! I know not what course others may take; but as for me, give me liberty, or give me death!"

While Henry used "slavery" as a metaphor, Colonists were enslaving Africans for real. And as they fought the British, many Americans fretted that the real slaves would wage their own revolutionary war—against the Americans. In fact, during all periods of turbulence up through the Civil War, Americans feared a revolt.

In his diary entry for November 24, 1775, future U.S. president John Adams touched on the subject. He had listened to two southern delegates to the Continental Congress, Archibald Bulloch and John Houston, who believed that the British Army might instigate an insurrection among the enslaved while waging war in the South. In a few weeks, Bulloch and Houston claimed, 20,000 blacks would leave their plantations and join the British forces. According to Adams, these men said that the "Negroes have a wonderful art of communicating intelligence among themselves; it will run several hundreds of miles in a week or a fortnight."

Outside of the occasional small-scale rebellion, no revolt occurred during the Revolutionary War. However, the Continental Army took some precautions. In April 1776, Major General Charles Lee urged Robert Morris to have regiments from the middle colonies ready to reinforce the southern front should an uprising by blacks take place.

Since fear of rebellion always permeated the South, it is not surprising that the tumult of war would accentuate those concerns. During the War of 1812, Mississippi Territory governor David Holmes appealed to a U.S. Army brigadier general for a large number of guns to protect his people against black insurrection. Holmes wrote:

> **Scarcely a day passes without my receiving some information relative to the designs of these people to insurrect. It is true that no clear or positive evidence of their intentions has been communicated; but certain facts, and expressions of their views have justly excited considerable alarm amongst the citizens. For my own part I am impressed with the belief that real danger exists, and that it is my duty to lose no time in procuring arms for the defence of the Country.**

At the turn of the nineteenth century, Southerners feared a calamity when France took control, from Spain, of a massive amount of North American land (approximately the middle third of the current United States). Liberty and equality had been themes of the French Revolution (1789-1799), and Southerners feared that France would spread seeds of abolition in North America. In 1801, Secretary of State James Madison instructed Minister to France Robert Livingston to inform France of the great concern the U.S. had over the French takeover of the territory. He told Livingston "to point to the unrest which would occur among the slaves in the Southern States, for they had been taught to regard the French as patrons of their cause."

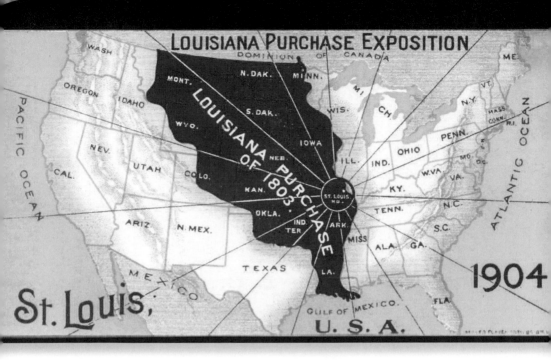

A postcard of the Louisiana Purchase Exposition

Again, no large rebellion occurred during this period of French control, which turned out to be brief. In 1803, the United States acquired this giant swath of land from the French in the Louisiana Purchase.

More fears brewed during the Texas Revolution (1835-1836), when Americans fretted that Mexico would spur blacks enslaved in Texas to rebel. In October 1835, a small uprising did occur. As a force of Mexican troops approached the Brazos River, a report stated, the "negroes on Brazos made an attempt to rise." The report noted that nearly a hundred blacks were rounded up. Some were hanged, and many were whipped nearly to death.

Any national, regional, or local crisis—not just war—was enough to stir fears of uprisings. Economic recessions definitely raised the rate of rebellion. The severity of droughts correlated with a fleeing of blacks. During times of drought, a slaveholder had to cut back on rations, meaning less food for the people he kept as slaves. They might also force his black laborers to work even harder. Such hardships angered blacks and gave them a greater impetus to revolt or run away.

Also, with fewer crops to harvest during a drought, planters may not have needed all the people kept as slaves. A few runaways would not have mattered much. In fact, it meant fewer mouths to feed. Moreover, the trading value of people who were enslaved plummeted during droughts, since fellow slaveholders also had an overabundance of black bondsmen and bondswomen and certainly had no need to buy more.

While blacks' opportunity for freedom rose during times of economic hardship, they generally did not fare well during such periods. Near the turn of the eighteenth century, an escaped man wrote: "I am convinced, that in nine cases out of ten, the hardships and sufferings of the colored population of lower Virginia is attributable to poverty and distress of its owners."

Chimney sweeps

Even though the prices for enslaved people were low during bad economic times, the selling of the enslaved increased during such periods. This often led to family breakups—a permanent farewell among loved ones. Also, more blacks were leased during a bad economy, and those who acquired leased "chattel" tended to treat them worse than the original owners had. Even if a black man or woman escaped during this period, he or she was undoubtedly hungry and malnourished, and then often became lost in hostile territory.

While slaveholders feared that the British and French and Mexicans would stir rebellion during times of war, their number-one enemy was domestic: the abolitionists.

Calls for the abolishment of American slavery dated back to the late 1600s, when Quakers condemned the practice. Abolitionist groups railed against slavery into the 1800s, but the cause did not gain full traction until the 1820s and '30s—around the time of the Second Great Awakening. During this religious revival movement, more and more Protestant Americans believed that the evil practice of slavery needed to end.

Around this time, many important abolitionist moments occurred. In 1831, William Lloyd Garrison and Isaac Knapp published the *Liberator*, an abolitionist newspaper. A year later, Garrison founded the New England Antislavery Society. In 1839, abolitionists formed their own political party, the Liberty Party, with James Birney as their presidential candidate. Unlike other groups that preached slavery reform, abolitionists demanded total emancipation. "Enslave the liberty of but one human being," Garrison declared, "and the liberties of the world are put in peril."

Free blacks were very much a part of the abolitionist movement. In 1827, the first African American newspaper, *Freedom's Journal*, was published. Two years later, David Walker—a free black originally from the South—published *An Appeal to the Coloured Citizens of the World*. It was an eloquent and forceful plea for the abolition of slavery:

> For you must remember that we are men as well as they. God has been pleased to give us two eyes, two hands, two feet, and some sense in our heads as well as they. They have no more right to hold us in slavery than we have to hold them, we have just as much right, in the sight of God, to hold them and their children in slavery and wretchedness, as they have to hold us, and no more.

What truly disturbed white Southerners was Walker's call for black rebellion. "[T]hey want us for their slaves, and think nothing of murdering us . . . ," Walker wrote. "[T]herefore, if there is an *attempt* made by us, kill or be killed."

Many copies of the *Appeal* were disseminated throughout the South. Walker, of course, became the most wanted man in the southern states. Georgia offered an award of $10,000 to any person who captured him alive and $1,000 to anyone who killed him. In the summer of 1830, Walker was found dead outside his shop in Boston.

Some historians have claimed that Walker's *Appeal* incited the biggest rebellion in American history—the Nat Turner Revolt—although that claim cannot be substantiated. Unquestionably, though, the buzz generated by Walker's words *coupled* with the horrors of the Turner Revolt spread panic throughout the South.

Throughout the 1830s, Southerners (including U.S. president and native Tennessean Andrew Jackson) often accused abolitionists of encouraging rebellion—a claim that historians have found to be more myth than truth. Though the abolitionist movement may not have instigated violent uprisings, it did offer a stage for free blacks to speak out against slavery. This, in essence, *was* rebellion.

The eloquent Frederick Douglass, who escaped from bondage in 1838, became the most famous black abolitionist. His written and verbal words were so powerful that they significantly swayed public opinion against slavery. He wrote:

What, to the American slave, is your Fourth of July?

I answer: a day that reveals to him, more than all other days in the year, the gross injustice and cruelty to which he is the constant victim. To him, your celebration is a sham; your boasted liberty, an unholy license; your national greatness, swelling vanity; your sounds of rejoicing are empty and heartless; your denunciation of tyrants, brass-fronted impudence; your shouts of liberty and equality, hollow mockery; your prayers and hymns, your sermons and thanksgivings, with all your religious parade and solemnity, are, to Him, mere bombast, fraud, deception, impiety, and hypocrisy—a thin veil to cover up crimes which would disgrace a nation of savages.

By the mid-1800s, the antislavery drumbeat was growing louder in the North. In fact, the United States was becoming a fractured nation, with a pro-slavery faction on one side and those who opposed it on the other. When western territories were primed to become states, political controversy always arose about whether it should be a free state or a slave state.

Prior to California becoming a state in 1850, fifteen states prohibited slavery and fifteen allowed it. With California admitted as a free state, Congress "compensated" the South with a number of concessions. One was the passage of the Fugitive Slave Act of 1850. This controversial law required U.S. citizens to assist in the recovery of freedom seekers who had escaped. Specifically, it made federal marshals or other officials who did not arrest an alleged runaway liable to a fine of $1,000. Also, a person who aided a freedom seeker with food or shelter could be fined $1,000 or imprisoned for up to six months. Officers who captured a runaway were entitled to a bonus or promotion. Captured blacks had no right to a jury trial.

An 1850 lithograph of the "Effect of the Fugitive Slave Law." A detail of the print shows four black men, who have been ambushed by a posse of six armed whites in a cornfield. One of the white men fires on them. Two of the blacks have evidently been hit; one has fallen to the ground while the second staggers, clutching the back of his bleeding head.

Many slaveholders applauded the new law, believing it would discourage freedom seekers from rebelling and running away. In reality, it was not that effective. The Underground Railroad saw its greatest success from 1850 to 1860, with many runaways choosing Canada, instead of the northern states, as their destination. Moreover, the new law strengthened the abolitionists' resolve to end slavery.

Meanwhile, a few noteworthy revolts erupted in the mid-1800s, including two that occurred at sea. The case of the *Amistad* mutiny would one day catch the attention of Steven Spielberg, who directed a motion picture on the intriguing episode.

In February 1839, years after the African slave trade had been abolished, Portuguese slave hunters abducted dozens of Africans in Sierra Leone. Though it was illegal to transport enslaved Africans to the Americas, it wasn't illegal to sell enslaved Cubans. Looking to get around the law, the slave hunters sent the Africans to Cuba, sold them to two Spanish planters, and put them aboard the Cuban schooner *La Amistad*. The intention was to sell these Africans as "Cuban" slaves.

The enslaved men turned the plot upside down. On July 1, after one of the *Amistad* captives found a rusty file, they freed themselves and staged a mutiny. They killed the captain and the cook and ordered the planters to head to Africa. Instead, eight weeks later—after many of the captives had died—the schooner was seized off the coast of Long Island, New York.

The Spanish planters were set free, and the Africans were imprisoned on charges of murder. But this was an extremely complicated situation. The defendants were not American. They had been captured illegally and were not technically slaves. They had killed two men, but only in response to being abducted. The case went to the U.S. Supreme Court in January 1841, and former U.S. president John Quincy Adams defended the Africans. He won, and the defendants were returned to Africa.

Later in 1841, another rebellion erupted at sea. That fall, the American brig *Creole* carried hemp, tobacco, flax, three passengers, and 135 slaves from Virginia to New Orleans via the Atlantic Ocean. Madison Washington was one of the 135 slaves onboard. In 1840, he had escaped to Canada but was captured when he returned to Virginia to find his wife, Susan. There, in Richmond, he was sold and put on board the *Creole*. Unbeknownst to him, Susan was among the women captives.

On the ninth day at sea, a group of blacks subdued the crew and took over the ship. Washington became its captain, and he ordered the white overseer to steer the ship to the Bahamas, a British colony, because Britain had outlawed slavery. At some point, Washington ordered the ship's cook to prepare breakfast for him and his comrades, and when they entered to eat, Susan appeared. The two embraced and wept.

When the *Creole* arrived in Nassau, Bahamas, on November 9, British authorities imprisoned the nineteen blacks who had participated in the revolt. As for the remaining mutineers, local residents escorted them off the ship and insisted that the British grant them freedom. Without any enslaved people aboard, the brig sailed to New Orleans.

The *Creole* episode developed into a complicated legal case. All the enslaved men—the mutineers and the others—were the property of American slaveholders. But British officials in the Bahamas ruled that local laws applied to the *Creole*. Because slavery was illegal in the British Empire (it had been abolished in 1833), the enslaved people aboard the *Creole* were declared free.

Southerners were outraged by the ruling. But in an abolitionist newspaper, the black resisters were hailed as "The Hero Mutineers." The story glorified Madison Washington, praising him for dressing the wounds of the sailors who had fought against him.

U.S. secretary of state Daniel Webster agreed with the British that the nineteen imprisoned blacks should not be tried for murder or mutiny. The uprising, he reasoned, had occurred outside of American jurisdiction. Moreover, he stated, the mutineers did not need to be sent to the United States, because England did not have an extradition treaty with the U.S. Thus, the black prisoners were both freed from all charges and freed from slavery.

Eventually, the slaveholders were compensated for their loss of property. Fourteen years after the mutiny, a claims commission ordered the British government to pay them more than $110,000 in compensation.

In Florida in the mid-1830s, blacks participated in what some have called the largest rebellion in American history. As with *La Amistad* and *Creole*, this is a complicated tale. At the time, American Indian groups collectively known as the Seminoles fought government troops in the U.S. territory of Florida. The Second Seminole War began in 1835 after the Native Americans refused U.S. orders to relocate to western lands.

Negro Abraham.

Abraham, runaway and
chief adviser to Seminole
chief Micanopy

Among the Indian fighters were men of African descent. This collection of Black Seminoles, which included free blacks and former runaway slaves, had established ties with the Seminole Indians and, thus, joined them as brothers-in-arms.

During the Second Seminole War, hundreds of blacks—perhaps as many as one thousand—escaped from their plantations and joined the Seminole Indians and Black Seminoles. Many of the enslaved painted their faces to indicate their new allegiance. Together, they helped the Seminoles destroy many of the large sugar plantations along the St. Johns River.

Though the Seminoles lost the war, the enslaved did not fare as badly as those in other revolts. At least ninety-three of them were captured by the U.S. Army and returned to their owners. There were no mass trials or gruesome executions. Some of the escapees joined with the Black Seminoles in the mass migration of Seminole Indians. Lieutenant Sprague of the U.S. Army explained why he was anxious to move all the black enemies out of Florida:

> The negroes . . . have, for their numbers, been the most formidable foe, more bloodthirsty, active, and revengeful, than the Indians. . . . The negro, returned to his original owner, might have remained a few days, when he again would have fled to the swamps, more vindictive than ever. . . . Ten resolute negroes, with a knowledge of the country, are sufficient to desolate the frontier, from one extent to the other.

This engraving depicts the "Horrid Massacre of the Whites in Florida" from December 1835 to April 1836, when "near Four Hundred (including women and children) fell victim to the barbarity of the Negroes and Indians."

No story of rebellion, or bravery, would be complete without the tale of John Brown, a zealous white abolitionist who spearheaded an uprising in Virginia in 1859.

Born in Connecticut in 1800, Brown grew up in a deeply religious family. His father strongly opposed slavery, and so did John. Into the 1850s, John Brown worked various jobs in the North, fathered twenty children, and found time to support the antislavery cause. He participated in the Underground Railroad, gave land to blacks running from enslavement, and helped finance the publication of David Walker's volcanically controversial *Appeal*. He and his wife even raised a black child.

Black abolitionist Frederick Douglass declared that, "though a white gentleman, [Brown] is in sympathy a black man, and as deeply interested in our cause, as though his own soul had been pierced with the iron of slavery."

In the mid-1850s, Kansas Territory became the battleground for a mini civil war. By law, the people of the territory could vote as to whether Kansas, when it achieved statehood, would be a free state or a slave state. Armed crusaders from both sides of the cause swarmed into Kansas. John Brown was among them, and he became a leader of antislavery guerillas. In 1856, in what became known as the Pottawatomie Massacre, Brown and his followers brutally killed five proslavery men.

Avoiding capture, Brown continued with his mission to abolish slavery through any means necessary. In October 1859, he raised a small army in a quest to eradicate slavery in Virginia. Actually, he had amassed (from abolitionist groups) more weapons than soldiers. He accumulated nearly two hundred rifles and almost a thousand pikes. His regiment included just twenty-one men: fifteen whites, three free blacks, one freed slave, and one runaway slave.

John Brown, in 1846 or 1847. The photographer of this portrait, Augustus Washington, was the son of a former slave.

On October 16, Brown led a raid on a federal arsenal in Harpers Ferry, Virginia, which contained 100,000 muskets and rifles. With his current stash of weapons and those he planned to steal, Brown felt he could arm hundreds of blacks in the area on the first night alone. In his mind, it would be the greatest rebellion of enslaved black people the nation had ever seen.

Brown's band did capture the armory, and then they rounded up dozens of townspeople as hostages. But the plan quickly unraveled when local militiamen, and the U.S. Marines under the leadership of Robert E. Lee, stormed the town. Two days later, after the deaths of ten abolitionists, one Marine, and six civilians, Brown was captured.

Brown was convicted of treason and sentenced to die by hanging. Before hearing his fate, he declared: "Now, if it is deemed necessary that I should forfeit my life for the furtherance of the ends of justice, and mingle my blood further with the blood of my children, and with the blood of millions in this slave country whose rights are disregarded by wicked, cruel, and unjust enactments, I submit; so let it be done."

John Brown's raid polarized the nation even more on the issue of slavery. Some southern newspapers labeled Northerners—and presidential candidate Abraham Lincoln—as Brown sympathizers. To many Northerners, Brown was indeed glorified as a martyr. In his lecture entitled "Courage," delivered in Boston on November 8, 1859, Ralph Waldo Emerson declared that Brown was "that new saint, than whom none purer or more brave was ever led by love of men into conflict and death—the new saint awaiting his martyrdom, and who, if he shall suffer, will make the gallows glorious like the cross."

While uprisings in earlier generations had sprouted and died, with no effect outside of their small communities, the big rebellions of the 1820s and beyond were impacting the nation. Nat Turner's revolt was well organized, violent, and frightening to the masses. David Walker's and Frederick Douglas's rebellious writings had a powerful impact on America's conscience. And John Brown's revolt gave Americans a sense that war over the slavery issue might be inevitable.

Whether or not he was a martyr, he was clearly prophetic when he declared, "I, John Brown am now quite certain that the crimes of this guilty land will never be purged away but with Blood."

The Robert Gould Shaw and Massachusetts Fifty-fourth Regiment Memorial, in Boston. The Massachusetts Fifty-fourth Volunteer Infantry was the first regiment of African Americans recruited in the North for service in the Union Army. Commanded by Robert Shaw, many of the volunteers had enlisted at the urging of Frederick Douglass.

"I wish there was some law here, or some protection. I know the southerners pretty well . . . having been in the service so long as a detective that I still find myself scrutinizing them closely. There is . . . that sinister expression about the eye, and the quiet but bitterly expressed feeling that I know portends evil . . . with a little whiskey in them, they dare do anything. . . . Do not think I am frightened and laugh at my letter. Anyone that has spent 4 months in Richmond prison does not be so easily frightened."

Mary Elizabeth Bowser,
freed slave turned Union Army spy

Emancipated and Armed for BATTLE

Previous American wars had put southern slaveholders on edge. As the Civil War began in April 1861, that edginess often turned to outright panic.

Such was the case in Southwest Mississippi in 1861. In May, citizens of Jefferson County hanged four blacks simply because, according to plantation mistress Susan Sillers Darden, they were "talking a great deal about Lincoln freeing the servants."

Such talk should have been expected at the time. Slave owners often talked to their friends and family about the Civil War and how President Abraham Lincoln wanted to free black people held in perpetual bondage. Black men and women often repeated what they had heard from their masters, or they discussed emancipation rumors that they had heard from fellow blacks.

An 1856 map showing free and slave states, with statistics for each of the states from the 1850 census, the results of the 1852 presidential election, and the number of enslaved people held by owners. The map is also embellished with portraits of John C. Fremont and William L. Dayton, the 1856 presidential and vice presidential candidates of the newly organized Republican Party, which advocated an antislavery platform.

To whites in Adams County (near Jefferson County), hearing the words *Lincoln* and *freedom* spill from a black person's lips was enough to sound alarm bells. Slaveholders in this area had grown exceptionally wealthy thanks to the forced labor of black men, women, and children, so they had a great deal to lose. More importantly, they were outnumbered by blacks by a large margin; a rebellion could have resulted in a massacre. Fears of a mass revolt, like in Saint-Domingue on the eve of the Haitian Revolution, were part of the public consciousness.

In Natchez, the Adams County seat, panic surfaced in September 1861 after large fires roared in the city. Planters formed a vigilance committee, whose members believed that blacks would "kill their masters" and "take the ladies for wives." Historians have found no hard evidence of a revolt conspiracy in the area. Nevertheless, whites went after black people with a vengeance. Days after the fires, ten were hanged on Jacob Surget's plantation.

A witch hunt mentality took over the area. Many black people were arrested. Their "testimony" to the "conspiracy" was extracted through torture. James Carter was accused of reading news of the Civil War to fellow blacks. Committee members "would whip [me] until I fainted," he recalled, "and then stop and whip again. Dr. Harper sat by and would feel my pulse and told them when to stop and when to go on."

According to noted abolitionist Laura Haviland, more than two hundred blacks in the area were executed by the time Union troops arrived in 1863.

Though an actual conspiracy may not have existed around Natchez, conspiracies and actual revolts did occur during and just prior to the Civil War. Across the North and South, tensions reached a fevered pitch during the 1860 presidential campaign, when northern Republican Abraham Lincoln ran against three candidates, including two from the South. In Winston County, Mississippi, a white man led an insurrection. According to the plan, blacks would poison all the whites in the county on Election Day, take arms, and wage war against whites. An enslaved girl betrayed the plot.

In Tennessee, a similar plot occurred—or at least was reported by Congressman John H. Reagan. He wrote that whites and blacks had planned

to poison as many people as they could on Sunday Night before the election, and on the day of the election to burn the houses and kill as many of the women and children as they could while the men were gone to the election, and then kill the men as they returned home. On last Sunday two white men, who lived up near Catfish Bayou, were hung as the ringleaders of the plot in this county.

Numerous rebellions, small and large, were planned during these unsettled times. In Texas, some two hundred black people were involved in a planned uprising in the summer of 1860. They plotted to wage battle against whites while en route to their freedom in Mexico. Several whites and more than fifty blacks were hanged in Fayette County, Texas.

In Plymouth, North Carolina, a number of blacks were arrested for an alleged conspiracy that involved more than three hundred people held as slaves. William S. Pettigrew wrote that the freedom seekers planned to "march towards Plymouth, murder & destroy all they might encounter on the road, set fire to the town, kill all the inhabitants that might oppose them, seize what money there might be, also what ammunition & weapons they might acquire, then take possession of such vessels as they required."

In Greensboro, Alabama, in 1861, sixteen black people were hanged on charges of insurrection. And in Monroe County, Arkansas, that year, two black men and one black girl were hanged for their involvement in a planned uprising. Rebellions and reprisals such as these sent tremors through the South. But early in the fall of 1862, a statement by President Lincoln rocked the region like a massive earthquake.

On September 22, Lincoln issued a proclamation: If any Confederate state did not return to the Union by January 1, 1863, he declared, he would order the emancipation of all enslaved people in that state. Southerners were aghast. Abraham Lincoln was attempting to shatter a way of life that had existed for more than two hundred years. After no Confederate state returned to the Union, the president issued the formal Emancipation Proclamation on January 1, 1863.

The Proclamation read, "all persons held as slaves within any State or designated part of a State, the people whereof shall then be in rebellion against the United States, shall be then, thenceforward, and forever free."

A parchment replica of page one of the Emancipation Proclamation issued by President Lincoln on January 1, 1863.

The order applied only to the ten states that were still in rebellion—not to the border/slave states that were not part of the Confederacy. In raw numbers, the proclamation covered more than 75 percent of the 4 million people held in bondage as slaves in the U.S. Practically, the emancipation could not be enforced in areas that were still in rebellion. However, in southern regions that the Union Army had already secured, the enslaved (tens of thousands of them) were declared free. Over the next two-plus years, as the Union continued to make gains through the South, more and more blacks were emancipated.

Historians have speculated as to why Lincoln freed black people from slavery. Some say he was morally opposed to slavery, while others insist it was more of a wartime tactic. Without blacks to tend the fields, the southern economy would suffer—which would cripple the Confederacy. Lincoln wrote in August 1862: "What I do about Slavery and the colored race, I do because I believe it helps to save the Union."

During the Civil War, slavery in the U.S. was not officially abolished, and former slaves were not granted U.S. citizenship. Those two dreams would become reality with the passage of the Thirteenth Amendment (December 1865) and Fourteenth Amendment (1868), respectively. In the meantime, emancipated blacks were called "freedmen."

In the early days of January 1863, news of the Emancipation Proclamation spread throughout the North. For many free blacks in the Union, as well as abolitionists, it was the fulfillment of a lifelong dream. Yet not everyone in the North was pleased. Working-class whites feared that huge numbers of blacks would flock to the northern cities and compete for their jobs.

Southerners, of course, feared for their lives. They envisioned emboldened blacks obtaining arms, joining forces, and slaughtering their oppressors. Addressing this potential problem, Lincoln had written in the Emancipation Proclamation: "And I hereby enjoin upon the people so declared to be free to abstain from all violence, unless in necessary self-defence."

89

For the most part, blacks did abstain from violence, but many "rebelled" by running away. Many headed to the cities, while others went searching for the spouses, children, and parents who had been torn away from them. On some plantations, former slaves ran off the owners. In other locations, they toiled in ignorance, unaware of the proclamation. In parts of Texas, news that Lincoln had freed those in bondage didn't reach the enslaved until 1865, after the war was over.

Incidents of violent revolts did occur from 1863 to 1865. In Lynchburg, Virginia, in 1863, five blacks were hanged for murdering their master. In Yazoo City, Mississippi, in 1864, blacks burned the courthouse and fourteen houses. During that same year in Choctaw County, Mississippi, slave owner Nat Best lived the nightmare that so many slaveholders had feared: the people he had enslaved restrained him and whipped him five hundred times.

In huge numbers, black men turned the tables on their former masters by joining the enemy, the Union—an act that can be viewed as rebellion on a grand scale. In the early years of the war, many escaped blacks fled to the Union Army for protection. They were known as "contrabands," and they worked for the Union as laborers and hired servants. To a large degree, however, these blacks were treated as badly by Union troops as they had been by slaveholders. A letter written by a committee of chaplains and surgeons, dated December 29, 1862, from Helena, Arkansas, stated: "The negro hospital here has become notorious for filth, neglect, mortality & brutal whipping, so that the contrabands have lost all hope of kind treatment there, & would almost as soon go to their graves as to their hospital."

Many free blacks in the North, as well as blacks who had escaped from plantations in the South, wished to join the Union Army. However, federal law prohibited blacks from bearing arms in

A washerwoman for the Union Army

the U.S. Army, and early in the war President Lincoln did not want to change that law. He feared that doing so would alienate leaders of the border states and prompt them to secede.

However, events in 1862 changed his mind. The number of white volunteers was dropping, the number of "contrabands" was rising, and the Union Army was in need of more troops. After the Emancipation Proclamation, the Union began to recruit black soldiers.

Black abolitionist Frederick Douglass was a great supporter of black enlistment, believing it would set the soldiers on a proper path. He declared: "Once let the black man get upon his person the brass letter, U.S., let him get an eagle on his button, and a musket on his shoulder and bullets in his pocket, there is no power on earth that can deny that he has earned the right to citizenship."

"Contrabands" at the headquarters of Confederate general Lafayette McLaws. Contrabands was an expression coined to describe escaped slaves.

Blacks burying bodies of fellow soldiers that died in the Battle of Cold Harbor, in Virginia. White soldiers and southern civilians often refused to bury black soldiers whose bodies were left on the field.

In all, some 180,000 black men joined the Union Army and another 19,000 served in the Union Navy. Approximately 100,000 of these soldiers were former slaves. In May 1863, Congress established the Bureau of Colored Troops (USCT) to organize black soldiers.

Within the Union Army, free blacks and former slaves faced severe prejudice. Fellow white soldiers called them racist names and sometimes physically abused them. Initially, their pay was less than white soldiers'. A large proportion of them served in "lowly" noncombat roles, such as cooking and manual laborer. More than 68,000 USCT soldiers died during the war, mostly from disease. USCT combat casualties were listed at 2,751.

When the Union won the war in the spring of 1865, free and enslaved black people rejoiced, for the triumph meant an unquestioned end of slavery. For black soldiers who served in the U.S. Army, the triumph was extraordinarily gratifying. They had not just killed a master, run to freedom, or burned a few buildings; they had joined together to help eradicate a slave system that had encompassed nearly a million square miles—that had held millions of black men, women, and children in bondage.

When Richmond, Virginia, the capital of the Confederacy, fell to the Union in April 1865, the Fifth Massachusetts Colored Cavalry entered the city on horseback and by foot. Comprised of free blacks and former slaves, these men, according to historian Benjamin Quarles, advanced "in neat blue uniforms, their shoulders erect, their heads high, their eyes confident." The freed slaves of Richmond ran along the sidewalks, admiring their new heroes. "In acknowledgment of their reception," Quarles wrote, "the Negro cavalrymen rose high in their stirrups and waved their swords. The cheers were deafening."

For former slaves in Union Army uniforms, the Civil War was the supreme rebellion—and the ultimate victory.

Group portrait of Company E, Fourth U.S. Colored Infantry, Fort Lincoln

TIMELINE

1619: Africans brought to Jamestown, Virginia.

1638: An uprising occurs in colonial Boston.

1663: Enslaved Africans and white indentured servants of Gloucester County, Virginia, conspire to overthrow their masters and escape into the wilderness. An informant foils their plot, and they are punished by death, beatings, and brandings.

1687: Another planned rebellion is discovered in Virginia. In the aftermath, the Council of Virginia bans public funerals of dead blacks.

1712: Twenty-five blacks kill nine whites and wound seven others by setting fire to a New York City house; within twenty-four hours, twenty-one of the rebels are executed by either hanging or burning. Six commit suicide. The South Carolina slave code goes into effect. It serves as a model for other colonies. Besides denying enslaved people all rights, such laws attempt to keep them ignorant, docile, dependent, powerless, de-individualized, and obedient.

1723: Enslaved blacks are accused of setting fires in Boston.

1728: In Savannah, Georgia, a large number of blacks plan to kill all the white people in the city. They gather together but do not have strong leadership. They run away when whites fire on them.

1729: In Virginia, black freedom seekers steal guns and ammunition and hunker down in the Blue Ridge Mountains. Whites attack them, killing some and returning the rest to slavery.

1730: African-born Samba Bambara is sentenced to slavery, for plotting to kill the crew of the ship on which he traveled from Africa. Crewmembers discover his plan, put him in irons, and break him and a few other men "on the wheel" once they arrive in Louisiana.

1734: A rebellious plot is uncovered in Burlington, Pennsylvania.

1739: On the Stono plantation, twenty miles southwest of Charleston, South Carolina, a rebel named Cato leads a quest to reach Spanish-held Florida, where the governor promises liberty to all fugitive English slaves. The rebels kill about forty whites, and destroy everything in their path, burning stores, taking up arms, and recruiting others enslaved on plantations. Nearly all of the rebels are either killed in battle or executed.

1741: In the New York Conspiracy, thirty black men are executed for allegedly setting a series of fires in Lower Manhattan.

1767: In Alexandria, Virginia, enslaved blacks kill several of their overseers with poison. At least four are executed.

1773: After Spanish officials issue a decree welcoming enslaved blacks to Florida, some twenty South Carolina blacks march southward, killing many whites.

1791: Upwards of 100,000 people enslaved on the French colony of Haiti revolt. The Haitian Revolution results in 200,000 black and white deaths and the expulsion of all remaining whites from the country. News of the rebellion influences similar revolts in the eastern United States

1793: The U.S. Congress passes the first Fugitive Slave Act, making it a criminal offense to help a runaway from slavery.

1795: In the Pointe Coupée Conspiracy, blacks enslaved in Louisiana plan a large-scale, murderous uprising. Though it never materializes, twenty-three alleged conspirators are executed.

Early 1800s to Civil War: The "Underground Railroad" helps tens of thousands of black people escape to freedom in the North.

1800: In Virginia, hundreds of men commit to a planned uprising led by Gabriel Prosser, a blacksmith intent on seizing Richmond and ending slavery in Virginia. The uprising never occurs, but more than two dozen people are hanged for conspiring to revolt.

1803: Angered that a black woman has been convicted of poisoning her master, blacks in York, Pennsylvania, attempt to burn down the town. Twenty are convicted of arson.

1805: In Wayne County, North Carolina, blacks plan to kill some whites through poisoning and—turning the tables—confine some to slavery. Three people are sentenced to death for poisoning whites, including a woman who is burned alive for poisoning her master. Many others are also punished.

1811: Slave driver turned rebel Charles Deslondes leads at least one hundred and fifty blacks on a march toward New Orleans. Sixty are killed during fighting and many more are executed.

1813: Reverend William Meade authors *Sermons Addressed to Masters and Servants*, which preaches that slaves should obey their masters because it is God's will.

1815: White storekeeper George Boxley attempts to free blacks in Virginia's Spotsylvania, Louisa, and Orange counties, but his plot is betrayed.

1817: A day after Easter, some two hundred freedom seekers riot in St. Mary's County, Maryland. Wielding brick bats and other makeshift weapons, they injure several whites before officials restore order.

1818: In Wilmington, North Carolina, seven enslaved blacks run away, raid nearby plantations, and kill an overseer. The leader of the runaways, Billy James, is never captured.

TIMELINE continued

1820s: An abolitionist movement begins to take hold in the North. Former slaves, notably Frederick Douglass, contribute to this movement.

1822: Denmark Vesey, who had purchased his freedom in 1800 and then started a successful carpentry business, organizes a plan to massacre whites in Charleston, South Carolina, and then flee to Haiti. His plot is foiled, and he and thirty-four others are executed by hanging.

1826: On a riverboat steamer in Mississippi, more than seventy black captives stage a mutiny. They kill five whites on the boat and escape successfully to Indiana.

1829: David Walker's *Appeal*, a denunciation of slavery, causes a major stir in the North and South.

1831: In Virginia, Nat Turner leads the deadliest revolt against slavery in American history, resulting in the deaths of some sixty whites and more than two hundred blacks.

1831-1832: People enslaved in Jamaica revolt, resulting in the deaths of two hundred blacks.

1833: Slavery is abolished in the British Empire.

Mid-1830s: During the Second Seminole War in Florida, hundreds of people enslaved on southern plantations join Seminole Indians and Black Seminoles in their fight against white oppressors.

1839: Captured Africans mutiny on the Cuban slave ship *La Amistad*, and the ship is subsequently seized off the coast of Long Island, New York. The U.S. Supreme Court rules that the defendants shall be set free.

1841: On the American brig *Creole*, nineteen of 135 people who had been enslaved in America take over the ship and sail to the Bahamas, a British colony, where they are granted their freedom.

1842: In November, black people kept as slaves of Native Americans revolt in the Cherokee Nation. They raid stores for weapons and ammunition, steal horses and mules, and then journey to freedom in Mexico. But they are soon captured.

1848: In Kentucky, a white college student named Patrick Doyle tries to lead more than seventy blacks to freedom. Armed with guns and other weapons, they set out toward the Ohio River. Local authorities engage them in battle, and most of the blacks are captured. Three black leaders are hanged, and Doyle is sentenced to twenty years in prison.

1850: The U.S. Congress passes the Fugitive Slave Act.

1850-1860: The South loses more than 100,000 enslaved blacks, valued at more than $30 million, on the Underground Railroad.

1856: Some two hundred blacks are found to have violated the law in a conspiracy in Columbus, Texas. Officials find guns, ammunition, and bowie knives in their possession. Three are hanged, and two more are whipped to death.

1858: Near Coffeesville, Mississippi, on the plantation of former U.S. first lady Sarah Polk, fifty-five enslaved people rebel because of the whippings they receive. They arm themselves with axes and other crude weapons, but a large group of armed men arrive to quell the uprising.

1859: White abolitionist John Brown is executed after trying to lead a large-scale revolt against slavery in Virginia.

1861-1863: Amid fears that enslaved blacks will turn on them because of the Civil War, whites in southwest Mississippi execute more than two hundred blacks.

1861-1865: Some 200,000 blacks, about half of whom are former slaves, fight for the Union Army in the Civil War.

1863: President Abraham Lincoln issues the Emancipation Proclamation, freeing people enslaved in the rebellious states.

Late 1800s to early 1900s: Some historians perpetuate the myth that enslaved Africans and America-born blacks were content with their lot in life and, by nature, docile.

1943: In his landmark book *American Negro Slave Revolts*, Herbert Aptheker finds records of approximately two hundred and fifty revolts and conspiracies that involved at least ten people.

SOURCES

Chapter 1: A Loyal Slave Revolts

p. 9,   "Brethren, arise . . ." Henry Highland Garnet, "An Address to the Slaves of the United States of America," http://www.blackpast.org/1843-henry-highland-garnet-address-slaves-united-states.

p. 9,   "being very severe . . ." Daniel Rapalye Rasmussen, "Violent Visions: Slaves, Sugar, and the 1811 German Coast Uprising," (bachelor's thesis, Harvard University, 2009), 37.

p. 10,   "horde of brigands," Ibid.

p. 10,   "Freedom or death . . ." Ibid., 91.

p. 10,   "On to New Orleans," Ibid.

p. 11,   "*un grande carnage . . .*" Lo Faber, "Slave Insurrections," ed. David Johnson, KnowLA Encyclopedia of Louisiana, Louisiana Endowment for the Humanities, October 13, 2011, http://www.encyclopediacms.com/entry/1121/&view=article.

p. 12,   "Their heads were . . ." François-Xavier Martin, et al, *The History of Louisiana: From the Earliest Period* (New Orleans: A. T. Penniman, & Co., 1829), 301, Google books online, http://www.books.google.com.

p. 12,   "foreign slaves . . ." Steven L. Danver, ed., *Revolts, Protests, Demonstrations, and Rebellions in American History, Vol. 1* (Santa Barbara, CA: ABC-CLO, LLC, 2011), 262, Google books online, http://www.books.google.com

p. 12,   "They are without . . ." Bedford Gaz, in a letter to a friend dated January 12, 1811, Louisiana Genealogy Trails, http://genealogytrails.com/lou/orleans/slave_revolt.html.

CHAPTER 2: Live Free or Die

p. 15,   "Let us arise . . ." Boyrereau Brinch and Benjamin F. Prentiss, *The Blind African Slave, or Memoirs of Boyrereau Brinch, Nick-named Jeffrey Brace* (St. Albans, VT: Harvey Whitney, 1810), 89, Documenting the American South, University Library, The University of North Carolina at Chapel Hill, 1998, http://docsouth.unc.edu/neh/brinch/brinch.html.

p. 16,   "They firmly believed . . ." "The Abolition of the Slave Trade," The Schomburg Center for Research in Black Culture, New York Public Library, http://abolition.nypl.org/essays/african_resistance/2/.

p. 16,   "[A sloop commanded . . ." Dorothy Schneider and Carl J. Schneider, "The West Coast of Africa: 1441–1866," *Slavery in America*, American Experience, Revised Edition, (New York: Facts On File, Inc., 2007), *African-American History Online*, Facts On File, Inc., http://www.fofweb.com/activelink2.asp? ItemID=WE01&iPin=AESch01&SingleRecord=True.

p. 16, "my boats and people . . ." Hugh Thomas, *The Slave Trade* (New York, NY: Touchstone, 1997), 405.

p. 17, "our natives, sons of the land . . ." Chinua Achebe, *The Education of a British-Protected Child* (New York, NY: Alfred A. Knopf, 2009), 64, Google books online, http://www.books.google.com.

p. 17, "We are warning you . . ." "The Abolition of the Slave Trade," The Schomburg Center for Research in Black Culture.

p. 18, "some white nation . . . thousand men," Venture Smith, *A Narrative of the Life and Adventures of Venture, a Native of Africa* (New-London, CT: C. Holt, 1798), 8, 10-11, Documenting the American South, University Library, The University of North Carolina at Chapel Hill, 1998, http://docsouth.unc.edu/neh/venture/venture.html.

p. 18, "with great firmness . . . six years and an half old," Ibid., 11.

p. 19, "You came to our country . . ." Brinch and Prentiss, *The Blind African Slave, or Memoirs of Boyrereau Brinch*, 89.

p. 20, "thought all our troubles . . ." John W. Blassingame, *The Slave Community. Plantation Life in the Antebellum South* (New York, NY: Oxford University Press, 1972), 7.

p. 20, "if he must be broke . . . Ibid., 9-10.

p. 20, "The water spirit . . ." Okey Maduforo, "Freeing the Souls of Igbo Landing Victims," *Daily* (Nigeria) *Independent*, July 10, 2012, http://dailyindependentnig.com/2012/07/freeing-the-souls-of-igbo-landing-victims/.

p. 20, "Every part of the world . . ." Patricia C. McKissack and Fredrick L. McKissack, *Rebels Against Slavery* (New York, NY: Scholastic, 1996), 13.

p. 21, "The old Hagg . . ." Karla Gottlieb, *A History of Queen Nanny. Leader of the Windward Maroons* (New Jersey: Africa World Press, 2000), 25.

p. 23, "I had to steal my food . . ." Ibid., 28.

p. 23, "I saw no prospect . . ." Blassingame, *The Slave Community*, 104.

Chapter 3: "The Negroes Are Rising!"

p. 25, "God's gonna set . . ." Baldwin H. Ward, ed., Pictorial History of the Black American (New York, NY: 1968), 25.

p. 25, "themselves to secrecy . . ." Jacob Ernest Cooke, *Encyclopedia of the North American Colonies* (New York: C. Scribner's Sons, 1993), 217, Google books online, http://www.books.google.com.

p. 26, "shot first his . . ." Saunders Redding, *They Came in Chains: Americans from Africa* (Philadelphia: Lippincott, 1950), 29, Google books online, http://www.books.google.com.

SOURCES continued

p. 26,   "slow fire . . ." Ibid.

p. 27,   "suffer the pains . . ." Daniel Horsmanden, *The New York Conspiracy, Or A History of the Negro Plot* (New York: Southwick & Pelsue, 1810), 80, Google books online, http://www.books.google.com.

p. 27,   "the detestable crime . . ." Allen Daniel Candler, *The Colonial Records of the State of Georgia, Volume 19, Part 1* (Atlanta: Franklin Printing and Publishing Company, 1911), 221, Google books online, http://www.books. google.com.

p. 27,   "an old sullen house negress . . ." Elizabeth Fox-Genovese, *Within the Plantation Household: Black and White Women of the Old South* (Chapel Hill, NC: The University of North Carolina Press, 1988), Google books online, http://www.books.google.com.

p. 27,   "the biggest devil . . ." Blassingame, *The Slave Community: Plantation Life in the Antebellum South*, 116.

p. 28,   "at the beginning . . ." David P. Forsythe, ed., *Encyclopedia of Human Rights, Volume 1* (New York: Oxford University Press, 2009), 399, Google books online, http://www.books.google.com.

p. 30,   "Shoot and be damned . . ." Kelly Houston Jones, "'A Rough, Saucy Set of Hands to Manage': Slave Resistance in Arkansas," *The Arkansas Historical Quarterly* LXXI, no. 1 (Spring 2012): 1.

p. 31,   "They hide themselves . . ." Forrest Moore, *A History of the Black Church in Tuscaloosa* (Bloomington, IN.: AuthorHouse, 2008), 57, Google books online, http://www.books.google.com.

p. 32,   "She meant to . . ." John Hope Franklin and Loren Schweninger, *Runaway Slaves: Rebels on the Plantation* (New York: Oxford University Press, 1999), 3, Google books online, http://www.books.google.com.

pp. 32, 35,   "in common . . ." Massachusetts Historical Society, "Petition for freedom to Massachusetts Governor Thomas Gage, His Majesty's Council, and the House of Representatives, 25 May 1774," Online Collection, the Jeremy Belknap papers, http://www.masshist.org/database/549.

Chapter 4: The Fear of a Black Revolution

p. 39,   "*Liberte, Egalite, Fraternite,*" Lerone Bennett, Jr., *Before the Mayflower. A History of Black America*, Sixth Revised Edition (New York, NY: Penguin Books, 1993), 112.

p. 39,   "In the eyes . . ." C. Jason Bromley, "Resistance and the Haitian Revolution," University of Miami Libraries, http://scholar.library.miami. edu/slaves/san_domingo_revolution/individual_essay/jason.html.

p. 41,   "It is high . . ." "Quotations on Slavery and Emancipation," The Jefferson Monticello, http://www.monticello.org/site/jefferson/quotations-slavery-and-emancipation.

p. 42,   "shall be held . . ." Ambrose I. Lane, Sr., *For Whites Only? How and Why America Became a Racist Nation* (Bloomington, IN.: AuthorHouse, 2008), A-59, Google books online, http://www.books.google.com.

p. 42,   "any slave, negro . . ." "A Brief Timeline of Georgia Laws Relating to Slaves, Nominal Slaves and Free Persons of Color," Coastal Georgia Genealogy & History, http://www.glynngen.com/slaverec/slavelaw.htm.

p. 42,   "'Druggists and Apothecaries' . . ." Ibid.

p. 42,   "was a pretty . . ." Peter Irons, *Jim Crow's Children: The Broken Promise of the Brown Decision* (New York: Penguin, 2002), 1, Google books online, http://www.books.google.com.

p. 42,   "If yer learned . . ." Ibid.

p. 43,   "police machinery such . . ." Frederick Law Olmsted, *A Journey in the Back Country* (New York: Mason Brothers, 1861), 444, Google books online, http://www.books.google.com.

p. 44,   "Now, when correction . . ." Harriet Beecher Stowe, *A Key to Uncle Tom's Cabin* (Boston: John P. Jewett & Co., 1853), 249, Google books online, http://www.books.google.com.

p. 47,   "I was never . . ." "Gabriel's Conspiracy," PBS.org, http://www.pbs.org/wgbh/aia/part3/3p1576.html.

p. 49,   "I have nothing more . . ." Robert C. Smith, *Encyclopedia of African-American Politics* (New York: Facts on File, Inc., 2003), 319.

p. 50,   "that the distinction . . ." William Pitt Palmer, et al, *Calendar of Virginia State Papers and Other Manuscripts* (Richmond: H. W. Flournoy, 1892), 433, Google books online, http://www.books.google.com.

p. 52,   "He was in . . ." Felix Gregory De Fontaine, *History of American Abolitionism: Its Four Great Epochs* (New York: D. Appleton & Co., 1861), 15, Google books online, http://www.books.google.com.

p. 52,   "Die like a . . ." David M. Robertson, *Denmark Vesey: The Buried Story of America's Largest Slave Rebellion and the Man Who Led It* (New York: Random House Digital, 2009), Kindle edition, chap. 5.

p. 53,   "return to the . . ." Thomas R. Gray, *The Confessions of Nat Turner: The Leader of the Late Insurrection in Southampton, Va.* (Richmond: Thomas R. Gray, 1831), 8, Google books online, http://www.books.google.com.

p. 53,   "I then found . . ." Ibid., 9.

p. 53,   "I heard a . . ." Ibid., 9-10.

p. 54,   "work of death . . ." Ibid., 12.

SOURCES continued

p. 54,   "we determined to . . ." Ibid., 11.

p. 55,   "It was then . . ." Ibid.

p. 55,   "he had only . . ." Ibid., 12.

p. 55,   "Vain hope . . ." Ibid.

p. 56,   "to carry terror . . ." Ibid., 14.

p. 56,   "in silent satisfaction . . ." Ibid.

p. 56,   "murdered Mrs. Waller . . ." Ibid.

p. 56,   "After showing her . . ." Ibid.

p. 57,   "Thomas Jefferson was the father . . ." Thomas Jefferson Foundation, "Appendix H: Sally Hemings and Her Children, http://www.monticello. org/site/plantation-and-slavery/appendix-h-sally-hemings-and-her-children.

Chapter 5: The Peculiar Burdens of Enslaved Women

p. 59,   "I had reasoned . . ." Sarah H. Bradford, *Harriet. The Moses of Her People* (New York: Geo. R. Lockwood & Son, 1886), 29, Documenting the American South, University Library, The University of North Carolina at Chapel Hill, 1998, http://docsouth.unc.edu/neh/harriet/harriet.html.

p. 59,   "Though we were . . ." Harriet A. Jacobs, *Incidents in the Life of a Slave Girl, Written by Herself* (Boston: 1861), 11, Documenting the American South, University Library, The University of North Carolina at Chapel Hill, 1998, http://docsouth.unc.edu/fpn/jacobs/jacobs.html.

p. 59,   "I now entered . . ." Ibid., 44.

p. 60,   "He told me . . ." Ibid., 45.

p. 60,   "slavery is terrible . . ." Ibid., 119.

p. 61,   "I was worth a heap . . ." Caroline Elizabeth Neely, "'Dat's one chile of mine you ain't never gonna sell'": Gynecological Resistance within the Plantation Community," (master's thesis, Virginia Polytechnic Institute and State University, 2000), 21.

p. 61,   "massa pick out . . ." Ibid.

p. 61,   "During slavery it seemed . . ." Ibid., 43.

p. 62,   "Hushaby, don't you . . ." Angela Davis, "The Black Woman's Role in the Community of Slaves," *The Black Scholar* 3 (December 1971): 9.

p. 65,   "near 'bout to . . ." Amrita Chakrabati Meyers, "'Sisters in Arms:' Slave Women's Resistance to Slavery in the United States," *Past Imperfect* 5, (1996), 160.

p. 66,   "we never goes to church . . ." Ibid., 150.

p. 67,   "I was thunderstruck . . ." Elizabeth Hobbs Keckley, *Behind the Scenes. Or, Thirty Years a Slave and Four Years in the White House* (New York: G. W. Carleton and Company Publishers, M DCCC LXVIII), 33.

p. 67,   "been the mother . . ." C. G. Parsons, *Inside View of Slavery: Or A Tour Among the Planters* (Boston: John P. Hewett and Company, 1855), 212, Google books online, http://www.books.google.com.

p. 69,   "The object of these . . ." Harriet Beecher Stowe, *Uncle Tom's Cabin* (Boston: Jewett & Co., 1852), preface.

p. 69,   "Its effect was amazing . . ." Hollis Robbins, "Uncle Tom's Cabin and the Matter of Influence," The Gilder Lehrman Institute of American History, https://www.gilderlehrman.org/history-by-era/literature-and-language-arts/essays/uncle-tom%E2%80%99s-cabin-and-matter-influence.

Chapter 6: Rebelling Through Words and Deeds

p. 71,   "O, that I were free . . ." Frederick Douglass, *Life and Times of Frederick Douglass* (Boston: De Wolfe & Fiske Co. 1892), 153, Documenting the American South, University Library, The University of North Carolina at Chapel Hill, 1998, http://docsouth.unc.edu/neh/dougl92/dougl92.html.

p. 71,   "Is life so . . ." "Patrick Henry: Liberty or Death!" The History Place, http://www.historyplace.com/speeches/henry.htm.

p. 72,   "Negroes have a . . ." Herbert Aptheker, *American Negro Slave Revolts* (New York: International Publishers, 1993), 21.

p. 72,   "Scarcely a day . . ." Ibid., 24.

p. 72,   "to point to . . ." Aaron Burr Darling, *Our Rising Empire, 1763-1803* (Hamden, CT.: Archon Books, 1972), 423, Google books online, http://www.books.google.com.

p. 73,   "negroes on Brazos . . ." Paul D. Lack, *The Texas Revolutionary Experience: A Political and Social History, 1835-1836* (College Station: Texas A&M Press, 1992), 242, Google books online, http://www.books.google.com.

p. 74,   "I am convinced . . ." Aptheker, *American Negro Slave Revolts*, 119.

p. 75,   "Enslave the liberty . . ." "William Lloyd Garrison quotes," SearchQuotes, http://www.searchquotes.com/quotation/Enslave_the_liberty_of_but_one_human_being_and_the_liberties_of_the_world_are_put_in_peril./56898.

p. 75,   "For you must . . ." David Walker, *David Walker's Appeal* (New York: Hill and Wang, 1995), 11, Google books online, http://www.books.google.com.

p. 76,   "[T]hey want us . . ." Ibid., 25.

p. 76,   "What, to the . . ." "'The Meaning of July Fourth for the Negro,'" PBS.org, http://www.pbs.org/wgbh/aia/part4/4h2927t.html.

p. 80,   "The negroes . . ." "Jesup's Proclamation," Rebellion, http://www.johnhorse.com/trail/02/d/29.htm.

SOURCES continued

p. 81,   "though a white . . ." "John Brown," PBS.org, http://www.pbs.org/wgbh/aia/part4/4p1550.html.

p. 83,   "Now if it . . ." Ibid.

p. 83,   "that new saint . . ." James M. McPherson, *This Mighty Scourge: Perspectives on the Civil War* (New York: Oxford University Press, 2007), 34, Google books online, http://www.books.google.com.

p. 83,   "I, John Brown . . ." "John Brown," Civil War Trust, http://www.civilwar.org/education/history/biographies/john-brown.html.

Chapter 7: Emancipated and Armed for Battle

p. 85,   "I wish there were some . . ." Lois Leveen, "A Black Spy in the Confederate White House," *New York Times*, June 21, 2012, http://opinionator.blogs.nytimes.com/2012/06/21/a-black-spy-in-the-confederate-white-house/.

p. 85,   "talking a great . . ." Justin Behrend, "Rumors of Revolt," *New York Times*, September 15, 2011, http://opinionator.blogs.nytimes.com/2011/09/15/rumors-of-revolt/.

p. 87,   "kill their masters . . ." Ibid.

p. 87,   "would whip [me] . . ." Ibid.

p. 87,   "to poison as . . ." John Townsend, *The Doom of Slavery in the Union: Its Safety Out of It* (Charleston, SC: Evans & Cogswell, 1860), 34, Google books online, http://www.books.google.com.

p. 88,   "march towards Plymouth . . ." Aptheker, *American Negro Slave Revolts*, 356.

p. 88,   "all persons held . . ." "The Emancipation Proclamation," National Archives, http://www.archives.gov/exhibits/featured_documents/emancipation_proclamation/transcript.html.

p. 89,   "What I do . . ." Abraham Lincoln, "A Letter from President Lincoln," *New York Times*, August 24, 1862, http://www.nytimes.com/1862/08/24/news/letter-president-lincoln-reply-horace-greeley-slavery-union-restoration-union.html.

p. 89,   "And I hereby . . ." "The Emancipation Proclamation," National Archives, http://www.archives.gov/exhibits/featured_documents/emancipation_proclamation/transcript.html.

p. 90,   "The negro hospital . . ." "Committee of Chaplains and Surgeons to the Commander of the Department of the Missouri," Freedmen & Southern Society Project, http://www.history.umd.edu/Freedmen/Sawyer.html.

p. 91,   "Once let the . . ." "Black Soldiers in the Civil War," National Archives, http://www.archives.gov/education/lessons/blacks-civil-war/.

p. 92,   "in neat blue . . ." Andrew Billingsley, *Mighty Like a River: The Black Church and Social Reform* (New York: Oxford University Press, 1999), 64, Google books online, http://www.books.google.com.

p. 93,   "In acknowledgment of . . ." Ibid.

BIBLIOGRAPHY

"A Brief Timeline of Georgia Laws Relating to Slaves, Nominal Slaves and Free Persons of Color." Coastal Georgia Genealogy & History. http://www.glynngen.com/slaverec/slavelaw.htm.

Aptheker, Herbert. *American Negro Slave Revolts*. New York: International Publishers, 1993.

Behrend, Justin. "Rumors of Revolt." *New York Times*, September 15, 2011. http://opinionator.blogs.nytimes.com/2011/09/15/rumors-of-revolt/.

Bennett, Lerone, Jr. *Before the Mayflower*. New York: Penguin Books, 1993.

Billingsley, Andrew. *Mighty Like a River: The Black Church and Social Reform*. New York: Oxford University Press, 1999.

"Black Soldiers in the Civil War." National Archives. http://www.archives.gov/education/lessons/blacks-civil-war/.

Blassingame, John W. *The Slave Community: Plantation Life in the Antebellum South*. New York: Oxford University Press, 1979.

Bromley, C. Jason. "Resistance and the Haitian Revolution." University of Miami Libraries. http://scholar.library.miami.edu/slaves/san_domingo_revolution/individual_essay/jason.html.

Candler, Allen Daniel. *The Colonial Records of the State of Georgia, Volume 19, Part 1*. Atlanta: Franklin Printing and Publishing Company, 1911.

Clines, Francis X. "'New York Burning': Gotham Witch Hunt." *New York Times*, October 2, 2005. http://www.nytimes.com/2005/10/02/books/review/02clines.html?pagewanted=print&_r=0.

"Committee of Chaplains and Surgeons to the Commander of the Department of the Missouri." Freedmen & Southern Society Project. http://www.history.umd.edu/Freedmen/Sawyer.html.

Cooke, Jacob Ernest. *Encyclopedia of the North American Colonies*. New York: C. Scribner's Sons, 1993.

Burr Darling, Aaron. *Our Rising Empire, 1763-1803*. Hamden, CT.: Archon Books, 1972.

De Fontaine, Felix Gregory. *History of American Abolitionism: Its Four Great Epochs*. New York: D. Appleton & Co., 1861.

"The Emancipation Proclamation." National Archives. http://www.archives.gov/exhibits/featured_documents/emancipation_proclamation/transcript.html.

Forsythe, David P., ed. *Encyclopedia of Human Rights, Volume 1*. New York: Oxford University Press, 2009.

BIBLIOGRAPHY continued

Franklin, John Hope, and Loren Schweninger. *Runaway Slaves: Rebels on the Plantation.* New York: Oxford University Press, 1999.

"Gabriel's Conspiracy." PBS.org. http://www.pbs.org/wgbh/aia/part3/3p1576.html.

Genovese, Eugene D. *Roll, Jordan, Roll. The World the Slaves Made.* New York: Random House, 1976.

Gray, Thomas R. *The Confessions of Nat Turner: The Leader of the Late Insurrection in Southampton, Va.* Richmond: Thomas R. Gray, 1831.

Harding, Vincent. *There Is a River: The Black Struggle for Freedom in America.* New York: Harcourt Brace Jovanovich, 1981.

Horsmanden, Daniel. *The New York Conspiracy, Or A History of the Negro Plot.* New York: Southwick & Pelsue, 1810.

Irons, Peter. *Jim Crow's Children: The Broken Promise of the Brown Decision.* New York: Penguin, 2002.

"Jesup's Proclamation." Rebellion. http://www.johnhorse.com/trail/02/d/29.htm.

"John Brown." Civil War Trust. http://www.civilwar.org/education/history/biographies/john-brown.html.

"John Brown." PBS.org. http://www.pbs.org/wgbh/aia/part4/4p1550.html.

Lack, Paul D. *The Texas Revolutionary Experience: A Political and Social History, 1835-1836.* College Station: Texas A&M Press, 1992.

Lane, Ambrose I., Sr. *For Whites Only? How and Why America Became a Racist Nation.* Bloomington, Ind.: AuthorHouse, 2008.

Lincoln, Abraham. "A Letter from President Lincoln." *New York Times,* August 24, 1862. http://www.nytimes.com/1862/08/24/news/letter-president-lincoln-reply-horace-greeley-slavery-union-restoration-union.html.

Lowe, John. *Louisiana Culture from the Colonial Era to Katrina.* Baton Rouge: LSU Press, 2008.

"Margaret Washington on the impact of the Stono Rebellion." PBS.org. http://www.pbs.org/wgbh/aia/part1/1i3079.html.

Martin, François-Xavier, et al. *The History of Louisiana: From the Earliest Period.* New Orleans: A. T. Penniman, & Co., 1829.

McKissack, Patricia C. and Frederick L. McKissack. *Rebels Against Slavery.* New York: Scholastic, 1996.

McPherson, James M. *This Mighty Scourge: Perspectives on the Civil War*. New York: Oxford University Press, 2007.

"'The Meaning of July Fourth for the Negro.'" PBS.org. http://www.pbs.org/wgbh/aia/part4/4h2927t.html.

Moore, Forrest. *A History of the Black Church in Tuscaloosa*. Bloomington, IN.: AuthorHouse, 2008.

Morison, Samuel E., and Henry S. Commage. *The Growth of the American Public*. New York: Oxford University Press, 1937.

Olmsted, Frederick Law. *A Journey in the Back Country*. New York: Mason Brothers, 1861.

Parsons, C. G. *Inside View of Slavery. Or a Tour Among the Planters*. Boston: John P. Hewett and Company, 1855.

"Patrick Henry: Liberty or Death!" The History Place. http://www.historyplace.com/speeches/henry.htm.

Phillips, Ulrich Bonnell. *American Negro Slavery*. Teddington, England: Echo Library, 2006.

Pitt Palmer, William, et al. *Calendar of Virginia State Papers and Other Manuscripts*. Richmond: H. W. Flournoy, 1892.

"Quotations on Slavery and Emancipation." The Jefferson Monticello. http://www.monticello.org/site/jefferson/quotations-slavery-and-emancipation.

Redding, Saunders. *They Came in Chains: Americans from Africa*. Philadelphia: Lippincott, 1950.

Robertson, David M. *Denmark Vesey: The Buried Story of America's Largest Slave Rebellion and the Man Who Led It*. New York: Random House Digital, 2009.

Stowe, Harriet Beecher. *A Key to Uncle Tom's Cabin*. Boston: John P. Jewett & Co., 1853.

Townsend, John. *The Doom of Slavery in the Union: Its Safety Out of It*. Charleston, S.C.: Evans & Cogswell, 1860.

Walker, David. *David Walker's Appeal*. New York: Hill and Wang, 1995.

"William Lloyd Garrison quotes." SearchQuotes. http://www.searchquotes.com/quotation/Enslave_the_liberty_of_but_one_human_being_and_the_liberties_of_the_world_are_put_in_peril./56898.

WEB SITES

Africans in America
http://www.pbs.org/wgbh/aia/home.html
This companion site to the six-hour PBS television series "Africans in America" examines the history of slavery in America from the start of the Atlantic slave trade in the sixteenth century to the end of the Civil War. It offers historical narratives, a resource bank of images and documents, and a youth activity guide.

American Memory: The African American Odyssey: A Quest for Full Citizenship
http://memory.loc.gov/ammem/aaohtml/exhibit/aointro.html
Displaying more than 240 items, including books, government documents, manuscripts, maps, musical scores, plays, films, and recordings, this is the largest black history exhibit ever held at the Library of Congress.

The Antislavery Literature Project
http://antislavery.eserver.org
Based at the English Department of Arizona State University, this site provides free online access to a wide range of the literature of U.S. slavery. It includes religious tracts and sermons, poetry, novels, short stories, historical and philosophical prose works, documents, and travel accounts.

Black Abolitionists Archive
http://research.udmercy.edu/find/special_collections/digital/baa
This digital archive of the University of Detroit Mercy is a collection of more than 800 speeches by antebellum blacks and approximately 1,000 editorials from the 1820s to the Civil War, providing a portrait of black involvement in the antislavery movement.

The Frederick Douglass Papers
http://memory.loc.gov/ammem/doughtml/doughome.html
The Frederick Douglas Papers of the Library of Congress is an online presentation of approximately 7,400 items, including images, related to all aspects of Douglass's life.

Gilder Lehrman Center for the Study of Slavery, Resistance and Abolition
http://www.yale.edu/glc/
The Gilder Lehrman Center for the Study of Slavery, Resistance and Abolition, a part of the Yale Center for International and Area Studies, is dedicated to the investigation and dissemination of information concerning all aspects of the Atlantic slave system and its destruction.

"I Will be Heard!" Abolitionism in America
http://rmc.library.cornell.edu/abolitionism/
Featuring rare books, manuscripts, letters, photographs, and other materials from
Cornell University Library's antislavery and Civil War collection, this online exhibit
explores the complex history of slavery, resistance, and abolition from the 1700s
through 1865.

Library of Congress--Born in Slavery Slave Narratives from the Federal
Writers Project, 1936-1938 American Memory
http://memory.loc.gov/ammem/snhtml/snhome.html
This online collection, *Born in Slavery: Slave Narratives from the Federal Writers'
Project, 1936-1938*, contains more than 2,300 first-person accounts of slavery
and 500 black-and-white photographs of former slaves. These narratives were
collected in the 1930s as part of the Federal Writers' Project of the Works Progress
Administration (WPA) and assembled and microfilmed in 1941 as the seventeen-
volume *Slave Narratives: A Folk History of Slavery in the United States from
Interviews with Former Slaves.*

National Humanities Center
http://nationalhumanitiescenter.org/pds/maai/enslavement/text7/text7read.htm
The National Humanities Center's "The Making of African American Identity: Vol
I, 1500-1865" includes texts of Henry Highland Garnet's "Call to Rebellion" address
of 1843, Willis Hodges's 1849 editorial "Slaves of the South, Now is Your Time!," the
1850 "Letter to the American Slaves" of the Cazenovia [New York] Fugitive Slave Act
Convention, and the debate in the 1858 State Convention of Massachusetts Negroes
on a proposal to urge southern slaves to "create an insurrection."

The Underground Railroad
http://www.nationalgeographic.com/railroad/
An interactive "journey" takes visitors of this site, created by National Geographic
Education, to stops along the Underground Railroad. The site also includes an
extensive timeline, maps, routes to freedom, fast facts, and profiles of abolitionists.

Virginia Runaways
http://people.uvawise.edu/runaways
Part of the Virtual Jamestown project, this site provides a collection of ads placed by
slaveholders searching for fugitive slaves. The site is searchable by gender, age, skill,
and other variables and is a project of the University of Virginia's Virginia Center
for Digital History.

INDEX

PHOTO CREDITS

All images used in this book that are not in the public domain are credited in the listing that follows: